W9-CMC-366

Contents

Introduction   ix

The Dimensions of Regret

Regret's Self-Inventory   3
1. The Regrets of Modern Life   7
2. From Self-Blame to Compassion   21
3. Wrong Turns and Roads Not Taken   41
4. Self-Deception and Regret   57

Journeying Through Life

5. When Regret Begins   75
6. The Regrets of Young Adulthood   95
7. Regret and Middle Age   117
8. Beyond Regret: Late Adulthood   139

The Challenge of Regret

9. Wealth, Fame, Power . . . and Regret   161
10. Coping with Regret   179

Appendix: Inventory Scoring and
     Self-Empowerment Worksheet   203
Chapter Notes   209
Index   213

Not everything that is faced can be changed, but nothing can be changed unless it is faced.

—James Baldwin

Introduction

Our goals in this book are to help readers learn how to avoid regret, to help them find the courage to confront regret honestly, and to help them cope with the feeling successfully when it appears.

There are also three major premises to our research: The first is that because regret implies personal failure, there is a sense of shame and even guilt about experiencing it. Consequently, most of us keep it hidden—from others, and even more (though often unsuccessfully) from ourselves.

We must break the silence that surrounds regret.

The second premise is that regret is a natural and necessary part of life. Because we do have only one life to live—life is not a dress rehearsal—a sense of regret or a fear of it necessarily plays a part in all our actions and choices.

We must place the experience of regret into a livable context, which means learning to live with it and, even more important, to learn from it.

Our third premise is that regret can be constructive as well as destructive; it can be used to fuel rather than restrict further growth.

We must work to convert regret into a tool for making positive life changes.

We hope that readers will use the experiences shared by

other people in these pages. Seeing what kinds of regrets touch men and women at various ages can help us avoid similar pitfalls when *we* reach thirty-five or fifty or seventy. The Self-Inventory that follows is another way to gauge your current level of regret and to introduce areas for self-reflection as you move through the book.

As Shakespeare warned: "To mourn a mischief that is past and gone is the best way to draw new mischief on." Instead, we can turn our eyes to the future. Using regret as an important part of the process, we can move beyond mourning and begin to make the most of our ongoing lives.

THE DIMENSIONS OF REGRET

Regret's Self-Inventory

Please complete the inventory before consulting the scoring key in the appendix.

For each of the following statements, choose the number that best represents your response and enter it in the right-hand column. Enter a "1" if the statement is not at all how you feel, a "2" if you feel somewhat that way, a "3" if you feel moderately that way, and a "4" if it very much reflects how you feel.

1 = Not at all   2 = Somewhat   3 = Moderately   4 = Very much

1. I wish I'd taken more risks in life. _____

2. I don't seek out enough new experiences. _____

3. I feel I've wasted too much time. _____

4. If I knew then what I know now, I'd have made some important choices differently. _____

5. There are some crucial things I've left undone in my life. _____

6. It's too late to make my life what I want it to be. _____

7. I fantasize about what my life might have been. _____

8. Things out of my control kept me from doing what I wanted. _____

9. I wish I had the courage to be more spontaneous. _____

10. I worry about what people think of me. _____

11. I'm critical of myself for things I do. _____

12. I wish I'd spent more time with good friends. _____

13. I wish I hadn't so often done what was expected of me. _____

14. I feel I've made too many sacrifices for other people. _____

15. I wish I'd lived my life more independently. _____

16. I feel cheated about not doing enough for myself. _____

17. I've made too many self-centered choices. _____

18. I've followed other people's values too much. _____

19. I wish I'd gotten more information before making big decisions. _____

20. I wish I were less impulsive in my decisions and actions. _____

21. I agonize over decisions. _____

22. I worry about decisions after making them. _____

23. I think about the career I didn't pursue. _____

24. I wish I'd balanced work and personal life better. _____

25. I wish my career hadn't taken second place to personal obligations. _____

26. I wish I'd taken more risks in career moves. _____

27. I wish I'd tried harder in school. _____

28. I wish I'd pursued my education during a different period of my life. _____

29. I should have gone for a higher level of education. ____

30. I wish I didn't feel responsible for other people's happiness. ____

31. I wish I'd married earlier or later than I did. ____

32. I wish I'd chosen my partner more wisely. ____

33. I wish I had (or hadn't) ended my marriage. ____

34. I wish I'd made different decisions about having children. ____

35. I worry about the mistakes I made as a parent. ____

36. I wish my relationship with my parents was better. ____

37. I wish I'd worked harder at expanding my circle of relationships. ____

38. I'm drawn to songs and stories of unrequited love. ____

39. I wish I had expressed myself more in certain important relationships. ____

40. I'm missing a really satisfying love relationship. ____

To score the results of your self-inventory, turn to page 204. It may be helpful to take this inventory before *and* after you have read this book.

Some time, when the river is ice
Ask me the mistakes I have made
Ask me whether what I have done is my life.

—WILLIAM STAFFORD

ONE

The Regrets of Modern Life

Regret, as a human and humanizing experience, connects us to one another by reminding us that we are all struggling with the limits of existence. As less-than-perfect beings in a less-than-perfect world, we try to make the best choices we can over a lifetime.

Poets and philosophers turned their lamps on the shadowy presence of regret long before psychologists made the attempt. Literature has also mined the feeling as a trenchant source of our universal story, for the prism through which humanity views experience is deeply colored by regret's poignant tones.

One reason for regret's being more the province of writers than psychologists is that it resists textbook explanation.

"A feeling of sorrow or a sense of loss over past decisions, dissatisfactions or disappointments" is one dictionary definition, while another takes a somewhat different approach: Regret is "distress of mind on account of something beyond our power to remedy."

Both definitions are true. Both are also inadequate.

Our own preferred definition of regret is offered by Pro-

7

fessor Robert Sugden: "Regret is the painful sensation of recognizing that 'what is' compares unfavorably with 'what might have been.' "

In fact, for every choice we make we give up a host of other options, which will always leave us open to feelings of longing for the options we abandoned. There are realistic gains and losses to every choice and, even more significant, a certain tragic loss in having to choose at all.

We can, however, resolve the pain of regret by understanding that both *"what might have been"* and *"what is"* are inextricable in the human experience. Used well, the pain of *if onlys*, wrong turns, and roads not taken can play a singularly important part in the search for a more meaningful life.

Regret is a hybrid emotion, a composite of many different feelings. People troubled with regret often confuse the feeling with guilt, depression, self-pity, or sorrow. In fact, regret resembles all of these, but it's also significantly different; unless the differences are understood, we run the risk of failing in our efforts to find relief.

• Regret often lurks in depression, but feeling regret does not make us clinically depressed.
• Although regret involves remorse and guilt, it is not synonymous with either feeling.
• As grief is a response to loss, regret shares much with sorrow, but it is more complicated than sorrow.
• While regret contains a dynamic of anger, it is more complex than anger.

Regret is slippery, elusive, subtle, multifarious. It glides in and out of our consciousness. We shudder from its ache, and grow exhausted from its relentless attacks. We try to hide from it, pretend it doesn't exist, call it by another name. At times our efforts pay off—something good happens, our self-esteem is restored, and we turn away from the past and the pain. But then we hear an echo of the past that reminds us of someplace or someone, and the feeling returns.

We can never know for certain what might have been if only we had chosen differently, acted oppositely, moved less blindly, but we can learn how to put much of the pain of those real or imagined "mistakes" to rest. No matter how stuck we feel in regrets from the past, we can direct our gaze and our energy to a future that is still ours to define.

André Gide once wrote: "It is a rule of life that when one door closes, another door always opens. Let us not, therefore, mourn so much for the losses behind the closed door that we miss the opportunities waiting for us beyond the newly opened door."

Some yearning for roads not taken is a natural part of life, but this doesn't mean we must mourn the past behind doors sealed shut with regret. When we focus too much attention on *if only* and *what might have been*, on how we might have reacted differently to some significant life event—on every error, failure, and missed chance for happiness—regret can become a way of imprisoning ourselves for these mistakes. And, as our energy is sapped by an impossible longing to rewrite history, we lose initiative to make the future better.

A paradoxical reward of regret is that it can be a source of liberation, freeing us from the heartache and guilt of past errors and miscalculations. The wrong turns we mourn can fire the energy to meet new challenges and explore new opportunities. Yesterday's lessons may have been hard, possibly even bitter, but with regret as our map, we can continue to grow.

In order to use regret as a positive force, we need to understand that the pain of regret is experienced as a continuum. In its mildest form the feeling can be a fleeting memory or fantasy, a pensive wish that the fates had been kinder or we had been wiser, but these regrets fade relatively quickly as we get caught up in currently satisfying experience.

Further along the continuum, as the experience of regret grows more acute, temporary disquiet turns into gnawing anxiety, diminishing our capacity to feel any hope or joy about the future.

At the furthest end of the continuum the experience of regret appears in its most painful, crippling form. We are mired in sorrow and anger at ourselves, and our very sense of self is seriously eroded. Because regret seems to have taken root permanently in our lives, we feel hopeless and despairing about its pangs diminishing, about ever knowing any happiness again.

Psychoanalyst Karen Horney wrote that the emotional pain people feel often reflects not just their inner struggle but what is going on in the world around them. When a great many men and women suffer from similar symptoms, she said, there is reason to think that "something is seriously wrong with the conditions under which people live. It shows that the psychic difficulties engendered by the cultural conditions are greater than the average capacity of people to deal with them."

That statement seems to hold true when we examine modern life and the experience of regret. Contemporary society intensifies regret because it claims to present us with apparently infinite opportunities. While having so many choices might at first appear to diminish the dilemma of regret—after all, we have so many routes to happiness from which to select—it has just the opposite effect.

Regret, which is inextricably linked to choice, has become a major malady of modern life. The more options there are to choose from, the more options we must relinquish at the moment of choice. As we choose more, we give up more, and create more "might have beens."

To understand our responses fully when we make certain choices or feel bad if we don't make them, we have to take into account what it means to be part of this particular time in history. Previous generations had far fewer choices than we have. For much of society, most children's lives mirrored those of their parents. They became the farmers or housewives or trainmen their fathers and mothers had been before them. If they dreamed of a different life, the dreams centered on limited, reasonably attainable gains over their parents' lives. They might, for example, hope to become a foreman instead of a worker, or be able to afford a larger house for their children than they themselves had grown up in.

As society evolved, for a variety of social and technological reasons—from a diminishment of strong institutional controls, to a more complex economy, to inventions like the birth control pill that changed the size of families, to expanded transportation facilities that broadened people's horizons, to machines that changed the nature of work, to medicines and surgical procedures that dramatically extended the life span—people began to see that their futures might be sweepingly unlike and infinitely fuller than anything known in earlier generations.

Today, the value of ongoing possibility and limitless expectations is deeply entrenched in our culture, and there is a relative absence of social and moral restrictions to check our desires. This can make us feel insatiable for new experience at any age. Our dreams can be intricate and unbounded, and our regrets over failed dreams may be equally intense.

There is another dilemma in a culture that heightens expectations about choice. We are confused not only about what we can do but about what we should want to do. Living in an age in which competitiveness and extreme ambition are common values can make us doubt and regret our genuine needs and feelings. Today, for instance, many women apologize for staying home with young children when they truly find great fulfillment in doing so. Similarly, both men and women feel self-conscious about not being driven to extravagant achievement, the better to acquire greater status and wealth and impressive possessions.

"Everybody I know thinks I should quit my job," says Paul, who is "locked" into a mid-level executive position at a large corporation. He sounds a little sheepish as he continues. "In a way I agree with them. I know I'm capable of moving up into top management, and that ten years from now it will be a lot harder to find a new position. I'm probably going to be filled with regret when I realize I no longer *can* move on.

But I'm contented here, and the salary gives me a reasonably comfortable life. I'd rather not risk losing the security this job provides me to try and earn more."

Although he had never thought about the relationship between cultural values and regret, Paul followed this admission with a wish "to have been born into a simpler time: when a man wouldn't have to be embarrassed about wanting stability more than an exciting career."

There is some evidence that more people are beginning to feel like Paul. They are choosing to live on a relatively modest scale, sensing that consumerism and blind ambition are not the definitions of a meaningful life.

For many other people, however, living in a culture that continuously whets the appetite for more causes an acute kind of yearning and discomfort. Being encouraged—even expected—to seize every one of our allegedly unlimited options only makes everything seem like enough. Cravings for everything unleashed, we resist the idea that *unrestricted choice is ultimately an illusion, that we simply can't do or have it all.*

It's understandable that some of us would have trouble accepting the idea of limits, because the notion of limitations does seem to fly in the face of cultural propaganda. As historian Daniel J. Boorstin explains, "During the last century great historical forces have promoted both the rise of images and the decline of ideals."

Surrounded primarily by images, he says, we grow further away from the genuine ideals that have sustained humanity since the beginning of time. These ideals, such as loyalty, equality, or altruism, are "perfect," but they are not "simplified" by being presented as examples easy to achieve.

By contrast, the books, magazines, and newspapers we read, the films and television programs we watch, offer us men and women whose lives are incredibly full of achievement. These media images of unrealistic lives threaten to engulf us with ostensibly accessible visions of glamour and fame, and actions without consequence.

We live in a culture in which almost everything seems possible. If we can explore outer space and develop human life *in vitro,* then surely we can play several roles in life and competently juggle myriad demands on our time.

We live in a culture in which the rapid pace of daily life prevents the kind of self-examination that could tell us what we really need, instead of making us so receptive to the seductive appeal of what we want.

We live in a culture in which an emphasis on personal gratification seems to sanction greed and encourage grandiose goals.

In Frederick Exley's novel about contemporary angst, *A Fan's Notes,* the narrator exclaims, "There's nothing I don't want! I want this, and I want that, and I want—well, everything!"

Although he is not a particularly distinctive person, Exley's narrator has extraordinary expectations. He dreams of "a destiny that's grand enough for me! Like Michelangelo's God reaching out to Adam, I want nothing less than to reach across the ages and stick my dirty fingers into posterity!" When he finally realizes that he will not even come close to his ideals, he virtually falls apart.

This passage illustrates another fundamental element of contemporary regret: *In a culture that worships success, failure is intolerable.* When we don't reap conspicuous rewards in a society that for the most part still promises everything, we hold ourselves responsible for failure. Clearly, we tell ourselves, we misused our freedom to choose. Clearly, our choices were "wrong."

Another element of modern life that creates regret is our confusion about the real meaning of autonomy and independence. We are supposed to be completely self-sufficient and never need to depend on anyone else. The price we pay for living up to this illusion is that we sacrifice the comfort and support of close human relationships.

In her novella *Rosa,* Cynthia Ozick writes about men and

women who left active lives in distant cities to retire to Florida. The reality of the transition was often harshly disappointing. For protagonist Rosa Lubin, for example, "it seemed . . . that the whole peninsula of Florida was weighted down with regret. Everyone had left behind a real life."

When we interviewed June in the sunny living room of her Florida condominium (she took a chair facing away from the beach-front window), she made it very clear that real life for her was still back in Chicago. A year ago, at the age of fifty-one, June was widowed. She explained that with her children grown, the family apartment was hauntingly lonely.

"One of my husband's much older ex-partners invited me to visit him and his wife in their retirement home in Florida. While I was there, they encouraged me to move down permanently. God knows what, at my age, possessed me to agree. Mainly I didn't want my children to feel they had to see me all the time, and I hoped that I could find companionship with these old friends. Boy, was I wrong! They barely have time for a phone conversation once a week, and they socialize with married couples their age who seem to resent my relative youth and freedom.

"So here I am, away from everything I value, in a glitzy condominium I despise, feeling like my soul and mind are withering in the sun along with my skin."

Her voice full of self-disgust, June described how she had ignored all the literature about widowhood that warned against making major decisions soon after the loss of a mate. "I can't blame anyone but myself for what's happened to me," she finished bleakly.

If June had been widowed in an earlier era, she would probably never have impulsively relocated. Choices for a middle-aged widow (and fifty-one would have been considered beyond middle age) were very limited. Her children would probably have felt a real responsibility for her care, and she would have felt much less compunction about accepting it. She would still have deeply regretted her husband's death, over which she had no control, but she would not have had to suffer what she condemns as the self-inflicted regret of severing all her major ties at once.

June's decision to move also shows the influence of yet another popular canon: Our culture places a premium on decisive action rather than on considered reflection about our true needs and values. In a state of emotional tension we often make impulsive moves that can backfire, such as making a phone call to a rejecting lover, or saying yes to a commitment we seriously doubt we can handle. Mainly, however, June's situation illustrates our contemporary preoccupation with independence. In an effort to appear self-sufficient during a time of genuine need, she cut herself off from a major source of emotional support.

In other instances the credo of independence manifests itself quite differently. We feel sanctioned by the culture to put ourselves first in a relationship, and often don't realize until it's too late that our self-centered expectations might eventually cause ourselves and others considerable pain.

Jeffrey is a stockbroker. "It's the damnedest thing," he says, his voice raspy as he paces the room where we conduct our interview. "When I was in college I went with a girl who was an artist, a little older than me and very nurturing. It was great at the time. I got a big kick out of her being so bohemian and such an earth mother. But when I got a chance to come to New York, although I thought about asking her to come along, I decided not to. I did care about her a lot, but she seemed all wrong for the kind of life I was heading toward. I felt a little bit like a heel, but she was so supportive and understanding . . . just like she always was about everything, that I was able to leave with a minimum of guilt.

"Well, listen. You know that big plane crash last month? She was on it. I was absolutely horrified when I saw her name on the passenger list. Then, by chance I ran into an old buddy from those days, and we got together for a drink. And he told me that Maggie had fallen apart when I left . . . she'd actually stopped painting and hardly ever went out. I couldn't believe it. Evidently, things did get better for her after she moved to Chicago, but you know," Jeff says, his eyes full of tears, "the newspaper said she wasn't married, and there weren't any children mentioned, and I keep obsessing about whether she was happy or not when she got on that plane, whether she was still hurt by what I had done to her. And all I hear in my head is my friend saying, when we first started talking, 'Jesus, Jeff, didn't you know how much that girl loved you?' "

Although Jeff's greatest regret is the tragedy of his ex-lover's death, and his callous treatment of her, another regret surfaced as we talked—one that also reflects a modern emphasis on career gain over personal relationships.

There have been many women in Jeff's life over the years, but no relationship has ever been really fulfilling. Now, in his late thirties, he feels a profound longing for a family and close intimate ties. He finds himself almost obsessively wondering what would have happened if he had made some genuine effort in his affair with Maggie.

"I got so much out of our time together, on such a minimal investment. If the relationship was so satisfying based on so little . . . my God! Imagine if I had really tried to develop it into something lasting!"

Another factor of modern life that contributes to regret is the unfamiliarity of the landscape of greater choice.

There are not always precedents for the choices we make. There is no clear standard to adhere to, no wise "elder" to consult. When our lives are so different from our parents', we can't easily look to them, or to the traditional social mores and religious beliefs they raised us by, for guidance in our decisions. When concepts of morality have changed so radically from those we were raised by, how do we judge what is right or wrong?

Many of us physically move several times in a lifetime, far from the places and people who shaped our early values.

Even if we do spend our adult lives in the communities of our childhood, or take permanent root in one new place, our choices for acceptable social behavior are historically foreign.

Micki, a woman in her early twenties, recently moved to Detroit from a small town in Michigan. Shortly after, she settled into a much faster-paced life than she was used to: "One night I spent some time talking with a guy in a singles bar I had begun to hang out in, and impulsively agreed to go home with him. Right away, when we got to his place, I knew I'd made a mistake. It was a fifth-floor walk-up, and he made me go up first. He started to play with my body from behind as I climbed the stairs. I tried to turn and go back down past him, but he blocked the staircase. I've never been so frightened in my life.

"As soon as we got into the apartment, he was all over me, tearing at my clothes. I managed to back away and started acting kind of coy, asking didn't he want a little music on while we got ready. (I had seen a stereo system along the wall.) He gave me a real angry stare, but I guess he figured I was going along with him, because he walked over to the turntable. The minute he turned his back, I was out the door and down the stairs. He came after me, calling me awful names, and I was terrified he was going to catch me and drag me back up again. Then, thank God, some guy came out of another apartment, and it was obvious he was suspicious of what was going on. While the two men kind of looked each other over, I bolted out of the building and into a cab that another miracle had left waiting at the curb.

"I still wake up at night in terror, replaying the incredibly stupid risk I took, and torturing myself over what could have happened as a result."

Micki's dangerous situation would have been nearly unthinkable in all but the recent past. Relatively few young women lived alone in a city, much less frequented singles bars. Micki was not "wrong" for wanting to exercise her new social freedom, but society breeds regret by making complete behavioral freedom seem both accessible and desirable. Given the reality of contemporary urban life, such total freedom is another, potentially very perilous, illusion.

Certainly people have always looked for ways to find pleasure or release from boredom and pain. (Dr. Samuel Johnson told a woman who complained that men became beasts when they drank, that there was a "strong inducement to this excess; for he who makes a *beast* of himself gets rid of the pain of being a man!") But modern life feeds this kind of behavior when it emphasizes instant gratification, and seems to promote artificial ways of achieving it. *Our culturally sanctioned desire for multiple and immediate gratification becomes a spawning ground for regrets that can last for a lifetime.*

Alcohol and drugs are widely available in every large city and even in smaller communities. We are enticed by invitations to take some substance that will help us relax, deaden anxiety, heighten our mood, promise spectacular levels of sexual excitement. A voracious desire for pleasure makes us extraordinarily susceptible to the self-absorbed delight of a drug-induced high. In one study of people working in the financial industry, 75 percent said they regularly used drugs at work, and 25 percent said they took drugs every day.

Long before many of these people find their lives collapsing, there are signs that their drug use is out of control. Many ignore the warning signals, however, because of the continuing myth that we never have to limit our desires. There is another important reason for avoiding the truth: the degree of regret to which the truth may give birth.

Charles, thirty-nine years old and struggling to rebuild a career on Wall Street, vigorously confirms research results indicating that the fear of admitting what the real cost of a long-term addiction has been can make breaking the addiction an even more formidable struggle.

"I reached a point where I desperately wanted to give up drugs, and I think I could have hacked the physical battle to break my habit. But as soon as I really tried to lick it, I had to look at the incredible waste I had made of my life. I had to acknowledge that I had just about thrown away some of the richest years of my early adulthood. I mean, for ten years my life was one goddam blur. How do you forgive yourself for that? How do you face the fact that you'll never get those years back? I'm doing it, but if you ask me what the controlling emotion of my life is still, it's regret."

You don't have to be addicted to drugs to feel the regret that Charles does as he faces his life. Modern society encourages a sense of failure when we fall short of perfection in any way, and so we hide the very human feeling of self-doubt behind a facade of false self-assurance. Because we are all supposed to see one another as competitors, other people are also afraid to let down their facades, and so regret deepens with our certainty that no one else is floundering the way we are.

"My greatest regret is that I'm not someone else," said Woody Allen. And indeed, any therapist will confirm how common it is for clients to wistfully compare themselves to acquaintances who seem to "have it all together."

There's the college roommate who's really happy with his chosen career, while our own choice is still uncertain. A long-time neighbor's marriage still seems vital, while our own barely functions. Another friend's kids are yuppie achievers, while ours are back at home with no goals in sight. A couple without children freely take off for exotic vacations, while our brief respites from parenthood are planned with all the tactical detail of a military maneuver. As we brood over our neighbors and colleagues, we continue to believe that it is still possible to live a life free of emotional conflict.

Accordingly, we measure our lives today not only by the number of high-powered roles we can play and the material possessions we can accumulate, but by the degree of regret we have about our own fulfillment or lack of it. How, though, does one gauge fulfillment in a culture that offers so many options?

The possibilities of unlimited choice become even more

confusing and alarming if we realize that we haven't really developed a personal value system to tell us why we prefer one option over another. Society seems to offer no clear standards with which to measure our impulses and desires as we face the common modern dilemma of choosing from equally inviting possibilities.

Choosing one delectable dish or vacation spot over another can cause some misgivings, but choosing among attractive relationships or intriguing careers can work against our actually enjoying the choice we make. With no fixed point of reference, we make our choices blindly.

"I had thought about being a history professor, or even a high school history teacher, before I drifted into science and ended up as a surgeon," says Howard, thirty-six. "No one in my family had ever been to college, let alone graduate school, so how could I really know what it was like to be in either profession? Now I've got financial success but enormous stress and, to my mind, very little creativity in my life. I don't care what people tell me about the limits of academic life; more and more, I long for it."

Howard is doing more than romanticizing "the one that got away," which is the common aftermath of most choices until we settle into them. He is gripped not just by a loss of opportunity but by what is very nearly a loss of self. The aftermath of his arbitrary choice of profession—and it is the arbitrariness that haunts him—is that he feels alienated from his own life. To his mind, being a surgeon is like being a high-powered technician. The antiseptic operating room has become a painful symbol of the sanitized emotional life from which he longs to be liberated.

"If only, if only . . ." Regret's pervasive refrain, stronger than ever as we near the end of this century of extraordinary opportunity. As we look out over the vast terrain of contemporary choice, we must step very gingerly over its potential land mines. *For choice without awareness and strong personal values brings more anxiety than freedom.*

We saw for a moment . . . the complete human being whom we have failed to be, but at the same time, cannot forget. All that we might have been we saw; all that we had missed.

—VIRGINIA WOOLF
The Waves

TWO

From Self-Blame to Compassion

Early in his career James Baldwin wrote, in the form of an open letter to himself: "You were born where you were born and faced the future that you faced because you were black and for no other reason. The limits of your ambition were, thus, expected to be set forever."

James Baldwin's experience is an extreme example of how regret is often inflicted on people by circumstances beyond their control. Had he been born into a less racist society, he would have had a far easier time developing and fully enjoying the fruits of his extraordinary talent. However, while Mr. Baldwin may wish that his life had been different, he can't blame himself for the pain he suffered because it was not.

All regret contains the wish that things were different, but not all regret carries self-blame.

Unlike James Baldwin's experience of racial discrimination, there are many situations where, whether legitimately or not, we blame ourselves for what goes wrong. Our recrimination is an important variable in the story of regret, for, according to Robert Sugden, *the amount of self-blame we feel for our regrets determines the intensity of our pain.*

Regret's link to self-recrimination is recognized even in cultures where personal choice is limited. In the Chinese language, for example, the word for regret is made up of two characters, *hui* and *hen*. The last character suggests frustration directed outward. We feel anger toward the external forces that impose capricious limits on our life. The first character suggests self-reproach—anger directed inward.

As with racial prejudice, when we experience the regret forced on us by oppression or other sorts of imposed conditions, our anger is primarily directed outward. No matter how great our pain, we know that no choice of ours precipitated our suffering. Because we understand that there are life situations we neither created nor can change, self-blame is generally lower at this end of the continuum.

For example: Our parents were bitterly divorced, and our childhood was bleak. We inherit congenital flaws that plague us with health problems. A mate whose protection we depended on dies prematurely. We are unusually short or physically awkward. We are the victims of some form of abuse from a hostile teacher, a sadistic camp counselor, or a tyrannical employer. We encounter the betrayal of love by a parent or other close family member.

Sometimes, however, even in these situations, we can later regret how we let them affect our attitude toward life, such as becoming immersed in self-pity or immobilized by anger. Or we actually may feel self-blame, perhaps because a severe religious or parental training has bred an obligation to assume responsibility for personal suffering. An important key to coping with regret is to understand when and why this response is inappropriate.

In the same way that children whose parents are going through a divorce must be helped to see that they were not to blame for the failure of the marriage, we have to probe our past to discover the real source of current anguish. It can be an enormously liberating experience to see ourselves, finally, as more acted upon than acting inadequately.

Eve's disquieting story illustrates this process. As a child she regularly visited her mother's sisters, who lived in a resort town. Like everyone else in the family, Eve worshipped one of the aunts, Christine, a beloved teacher and pillar of her church who, even though long dead, is today "still the official saint of the family."

"I was a very fat kid," Eve tells us, "and probably at my heaviest that thirteenth summer when I met Joey, a local boy who was part of my cousin's group of friends who spent all their time together. I'd been teased all my life by other kids, especially boys, so that I dreaded seeing them in any situation. My cousin practically forced me to come along with him one night when his crowd was going to the movies, and I couldn't believe it but Joey sort of singled me out. He thought something I said was really funny and sat next to me at the movie and really seemed to like me. I could always make him laugh, and he thought I was fun and easy to talk to, and he seemed to like me as a girl, not just as a friend, even though I was fat.

"For two weeks we were like a couple in the group. When we went bowling we were always partners—things like that—and if we'd go out for a hamburger with everyone, for the first time I didn't feel self-conscious. I still remember how good it felt to be just a normal teenager, with a bunch of friends and a special boyfriend of my own."

Eve confided to her aunt Christine how happy and excited she was about her first boyfriend, and her aunt obviously shared in her delight. "Then, one morning when I went down to breakfast, Aunt Christine handed me a letter from Joey. With a big smile on her face she told me he had just brought it by. My first love letter—and it was a poem, no less! It started out sounding like a romantic verse on a greeting card, but then all of a sudden it changed. All I can remember now is the last line: 'but you're too fat for me!' "

Eve was inconsolable, despite her aunt's attempts to calm her. Finally Christine suggested that Eve return home to save herself embarrassment. Over the years, when she was forced to visit her aunts again, Eve constantly avoided the possibility of running into Joey, and the one time she did, "although he was very responsive, I couldn't even look him in the eye, I was still so humiliated. . . .

"It may sound dramatic, but I feel that his rejection was really a pivotal event in how I looked at the world, and males in particular, from then on. I was even more awkward socially than I had been before, and became a lonely and reclusive adolescent. Obviously, it wasn't just this experience that made me have problems, but it certainly contributed a lot to my insecurity and mistrust of men. Well into adulthood, even when I was successful professionally and had finally dieted successfully enough to be in a range of normal weight, I couldn't form intimate relationships with men because of a fear that if I put on any weight they would leave me. My weight was always fluctuating up and down, and I constantly linked how I looked with how I felt about myself."

Last spring, eighteen years after she received the note, Eve discovered an almost inconceivable truth. "Ironically, it was at my aunt Christine's funeral. One of my cousins told me that it was Aunt Christine, not Joey, who wrote the note to me. No one could explain to me why she did it, other than that she was very religious and puritanical, and although none of the family knew it then, she was having marital problems that summer. Who knows? Maybe she was jealous. How can anyone understand such irrational behavior?

"I have never gotten a satisfactory explanation of why my cousins or other aunts never told me the truth before. I guess they were really afraid of Christine—for reasons that had to do with their own problems, not mine.

"In any case, after the initial shock and indescribable rage," she continued, "I'm discovering that this terrible knowledge has actually helped my struggle toward self-acceptance. Not just because I realize Joey didn't actually reject me, but I see with great clarity that at some level I *chose* to allow a bad experience to dominate *all* my experience. Maybe it's because Christine's act was so absolutely random, and so obviously out of my control, that I could understand how important it is to focus your attitude on more than what terrible thing has happened to you.

"Consequently, I feel I am ready at last to stop wasting so much energy regretting that I was born heavyset instead of willowy—most of all toward stopping this belief that how I look is the only key to my self-worth."

Eve is certainly not over her justifiable anger and the "terrible sense of waste . . . all those years of hating myself, tearing myself down. For months after I found out the truth, I couldn't stop obsessing about what might have happened if I'd known earlier. After all, Joey did make overtures when I saw him again. We might have picked things up, maybe even seen the relationship develop into something lasting. And even if it didn't, if I'd known the truth I would at least have known that Joey liked me even though I was fat . . . that I had something to offer him besides how I looked, and maybe I would have realized that if this was true with him, it could be so with other men.

"I also wish now," she continued thoughtfully, "that even though I didn't know the truth when I ran into him, I had had the courage to respond to his warmth, or even to confront him and demand an explanation for what I thought was his act of cruelty. I wish I hadn't been so passive in the face of abuse. But even more than I regret the abuse, I regret the way I allowed it to turn me against myself.

"Actually," she concludes with a sigh and a smile, "I've given up all this kind of replaying the past—at least most of the time. I feel real compassion for myself for having been the victim of a sick mind. And it's made me want to try as hard as possible to feel better about myself in general, even to bite the bullet and finally start trying to build good relationships with men."

Eve's regret lessened considerably when she stopped

blaming herself for what she lacked in life, and for how she allowed the lacks to affect her. She also learned that *while it is tempting to remain bitter over regrets caused by injustice, giving in to that impulse can cripple us even more.*

In psychotherapy, there comes an important point when, armed with self-knowledge and awareness of the roots of our problems, we have to make a conscious decision to move beyond the hurts of the past. The pain of her accumulated regrets had brought Eve to a point where she finally resolved to focus on her future instead of her past and, rid of the past's bitter memories, to go out and seek a measure of fulfillment she'd never known before.

But this task of letting go, of using regret to fuel a determination to live in a manner that deflects future pain, becomes progressively more difficult as self-blame increases along the continuum of regret. The possibilities for self-recrimination can seem infinite. "Why did I let that job opportunity slip by? Why did I put up with such abuse for so long?" And, sometimes the most quintessentially painful, "Why didn't I make the most of my relationship while it was still possible?"

When a person we love dies, a family member, friend, or mate, we are naturally devastated by helpless grief and the deepest level of regret. The natural regret caused by this inevitable experience is, however, greatly intensified when, along with our loneliness and loss, we mourn the quality of the relationship that has now ended. Whether standing at the graveside or lying sleepless in bed years later, the conviction that something was left unresolved stirs wrenching memories and a fierce, tormenting desire to undo what was done—or do what we left undone.

"The last time I saw my father I was getting ready to move to L.A.," Louise told us. "I was storing some of my things at my parents' house, and my father was following me around, making suggestions. He kept hinting very broadly that he thought I was making a mistake, that at my parents' age they weren't going to be able to travel back and forth so easily, and we would hardly ever see each other . . . thoughts I didn't need to hear from him as I agonized over my own doubts.

"Just because I *was* so freaked out about what I was doing, I took all my anxiety out on him, accusing him of being selfish and thinking of himself rather than about what was good for me. I knew I was being a jerk even while I was raving and ranting—both my parents were always exceptionally open, giving people—and I finally stormed out of the house without kissing him goodbye.

"Four days after I arrived in California, the call came from my sister that Dad had died of a heart attack. I'm not so egocentric that I thought it was because of my aggravating him that last afternoon, but I *was* absolutely in despair over the idea of his dying with the image of me as an ungrateful and uncaring daughter."

We interviewed Louise after she had already had the benefit of therapy, which had helped her see the situation, and herself, more realistically. She had begun to consider some other possibilities than the dark scenario she first drew. She would never know for sure what her father's real feelings were, but she was able to put some of her regret to rest by placing her confrontation with him in the broader context of a lifetime of many more good than bad experiences.

It is very common to feel that other people must react the same way we do to personal exchanges and events. Since Louise had felt so bad about their last meeting, she could not imagine that her father hadn't as well. In reality, everyone brings his or her own perspective to any experience. (How many times have you felt someone was resentful or patronizing as a result of something you'd said, only to find out later that the response had grown out of a fight with a lover or a boss, or any one of a score of possibilities that had nothing to do with you?)

Louise has come to believe that her father was sensitive enough to realize full well how frightened and pressured she was feeling that morning, and had accepted her bad temper with a father's understanding. She realizes, too, that even if he had been upset with her manner, the unhappy meeting would not cancel out a lifetime of mutual love and respect. Had her father not died so suddenly and unexpectedly, Louise undoubtedly would have quickly made amends, but it was knowing that she would never have this opportunity that escalated her regret into overwhelming proportions.

"Thank God, my counselor has helped me to stop blaming myself so unrelentingly," Louise said with a sigh. She is greatly relieved at feeling less culpable, but she also feels that her regret has made an important constructive contribution to the rest of her life.

"I'll never again put off making things right when I feel I have hurt someone unduly. Nor will I let any relationship drift into some stupid unresolved feud, as I've done once or twice with friends. I wanted to call Dad the minute I arrived in L.A., to apologize, but I was still feeling resentful that he hadn't bent over backwards, telling me what a wonderful move I was making. I've discovered the hard way that you resolve interpersonal problems while there is still time."

Robert is at a point much further along than Louise on regret's continuum, where he is plagued by even more unnecessary self-blame. He would not blame himself for a storm that left him feeling powerless during a turbulent plane ride, yet he cannot see that certain unhappy experiences in his life, like the weather, were simply out of his control.

With his wife Sara's complete approval, Robert accepted a coveted six-month assignment in London. Sara's own career demands made it impossible for her to join him, but she assured Robert that she genuinely wanted him to take advantage of the truly superb opportunity.

Two months into the separation Sara had to have emergency gynecological surgery, including a hysterectomy. She will never be able to have children, and Robert blames himself for her loss. He feels that he should never have taken an assignment that left Sara on her own—as if that could have prevented her illness.

The tendency to link self-blame to regret is amazingly strong, even when it is clearly illogical. From a particular point of view, we can hold ourselves responsible for absolutely everything that goes wrong. If a friend doesn't call us anymore, we're certain we hurt her feelings. If there's a mixup over a lunch date, we rush to apologize for the mistake. It would never even occur to a person governed by self-reproach that the other person might have gotten the arrangements wrong. Our own judgments against ourselves are remarkably resistant to reason.

It is completely irrational for Robert to hold himself responsible for his wife's illness. Sara's an intelligent young woman who takes good care of her own needs. Her emergency surgery had nothing to do with any recklessness or ignorance that Robert's presence could have corrected.

On the other hand, in some cases *an action taken or not taken does change the course of our lives, fueling even more the tendency toward self-blame.*

"So I'll have my degree. So what?" Jennifer comments bleakly on her decision to return to college in her mid-thirties. "I'll be close to forty by the time I graduate. It's not the same as having these credentials at twenty—I should have finished school when I had a chance to really build a career."

Jennifer's classmates of many ages admire her fierce dedication to learning, and envy her consistently high grades. She gets little pleasure out of her achievements; they are overshadowed by her regret at having left college to get married.

At the time she left college, her decision seemed like the right one for a variety of reasons. "But," Jennifer says, now juggling family and school responsibilities with a part-time job to help finance her education, "if I had known how difficult it was going to be to finish school later on, I would never have left college when I did."

Jennifer feels defeated about her life, even though it is clearly on the upswing, because she so deeply regrets a past decision that turned out to have a negative effect on her future. Like a detective with a magnifying glass, she seems intent upon finding her life's flaws, and her findings are always self-incriminating.

Jennifer hadn't recognized how much a part self-blame was playing in her feelings of depression. When, with the help of a support group, she began to see how harshly she was judging herself for her early choice, she slowly came to accept that her decision had some positive effects that she had overlooked. For example, despite the fact that having children had restricted her in some ways, she loved them deeply and had been able to enjoy them while she was still young.

What's more, while she will indeed be forty when she finishes college, her children will be well on their way in the world, and she will have far fewer family obligations than other women her age who are starting a career. She was also able to admit that she is a much better student as an older person, and gets much more out of her learning than she would have at eighteen or twenty. Most important, she understands now that at the time she decided to leave school and get married, she genuinely thought she was making the right choice. This knowledge has helped Jennifer to let go of much of her self-blame and her sorrow over lost time, and get on with her life.

Regret becomes much less intense when we look back on a decision and recognize that there was good reason to think we were making the right choice at that particular time.

If we believe we made some attempt to consider all our options and all their consequences at the time of decision, our regret becomes much less overwhelming, even if we turn out to have been wrong. This keeps us from the furthest end of the continuum, where, as self-blame expands, our regret reaches obsessive proportions. Here, where we relentlessly review our history to explain our current state of despair, we brood most bitterly over what we should or should not have done, hate ourselves for what we didn't but should have said, or panic over the possible effects (all disastrous) of what we actually do or say.

Wishing to undo what has been done, to obliterate the beginning that brought us to what seems such a catastrophic end, we wind up feeling like Lady Macbeth, desperate to wash our hands of the past. Unfortunately, although therapists often see clients who suffer this way, they don't always identify regret as a major factor in their distress. Particularly since the term *regret* is not common to the clinical vocabulary, its presence is often overlooked in people's stories of frustration, depression, or hopelessness.

What these stories do invariably reveal is that when *there is real evidence that we knew a choice was the wrong one at the time we made it,* sorrow over life's disappointments becomes a crippling rage, aimed at ourselves and our mistakes. Linda's story clearly illustrates this most crucial aspect of regret, the anguish that comes from knowing that *at the moment of choice, we really are aware that the decision we're making is wrong.*

Linda is exhausted by sleepless nights, agonizing over past decisions that have left her life bleak and oppressively burdened. She is recently divorced from a man she first met in high school. Although they had broken up four times over the course of their relationship, they finally married after she graduated from college. Linda's voice is shrill as she reveals that she always felt misgivings about their future together.

"I guess I was still carrying around the image of him as the high school hero. . . . It was such a big coup to have been his girlfriend. And he is extremely handsome. . . . I loved having people envy my being with him when we were out

together. Also," she says with a disparaging grimace, "everyone I knew was getting married, and there wasn't anyone else
on the scene. . . .

"But we never really had anything in common, and that
issue just kept getting worse and worse. I wanted so much
more in my life than he did. So what did I do? I compounded
the problem by having two children, one right after the other.
Now I'm not only divorced, I'm a single parent. A poor single
parent—he has very little money to contribute to our support.
If I had only paid attention to my instincts, and even my head,"
she accuses herself, "I knew from the very beginning that it
couldn't work out."

All of us are prone to ignore information that might prevent us from having or pursuing something we want. Whether
it's an exciting but imprudent business investment or, as in
Linda's case, a relationship that serves some dysfunctional need,
we sometimes move ahead without allowing ourselves full
awareness of the true situation.

It's important to realize, however, that when we are finally confronted with the consequences of our impulsive behavior (and sooner or later these consequences will almost
certainly appear), regret will be infinitely more intense because we will also feel culpable for willful blindness.

Whatever the cause of our regret and self-reproach, the
inability to accept mistakes as an unalterable fact of life can
leave us paralyzed. Further movement or growth seems impossible, *unless we can convert the anger at ourselves into self-
compassion.*

Self-compassion is the opposite of self-blame. *It is the key
to understanding and coping with regret, and helps us turn regret
into a constructive force.*

Self-compassion means, first, that we are conscious of the
fact that human beings all have their limitations (even if we
don't like it) and that we cannot foresee or control everything
that happens in our lives. It also implies that we can accept

ourselves at the deepest personal and emotional levels, with all our mistakes and limitations.

There is one primary and overwhelming obstacle to turning self-recrimination into self-compassion and ultimately into self-forgiveness, so that we can move on with our lives. The obstacle is contained in what may be the mind's most outrageous assumption—that it is really possible to be *perfect*.

Karen Horney linked the drive for perfection to what she called "The Tyranny of the Shoulds." Chased by images of what we should and ought to be, we believe that nothing should be impossible. No relationship should be beyond our control. We can/should handle every competing challenge and conflicting demand. Obstacles that limit the accomplishments of lesser mortals (such as a twenty-four-hour day!) should leave us untouched. To narrow our aspirations in any way is a cowardly, indefensible compromise.

We think we should be able to (to name just a few):

> always look wonderful;
> never make mistakes;
> be the best at our job;
> be the ideal lover, parent, or mate;
> be the most devoted son or daughter;
> handle every challenge easily;
> be liked by everyone;
> make everyone around us happy;
> and, the ultimate *should* of all, always be happy
> ourselves.

To complicate matters, we often don't recognize our need for perfection. "Who, me? Look at my housekeeping . . . my grades . . . my job history . . . my kids . . . my marriage . . . my weight . . . ! If I cared about perfection, could I live like this?"

In reality, *perfectionism has much less to do with how well we do things than with how well we—consciously or unconsciously—*

want to do them. Perfectionism, and regret over not achieving it, is a story of intent, not of action.

We all have what Horney called an *idealized image.* This is the self we think we should be but which, because it is perfectionistic, is unattainable. It begins to take form in childhood, when we seek the approval of people, usually our parents, whom we dependently love and whose love we desperately need. As we try to reach this idealized—or false—self, we become more and more alienated from our "real selves."

Trying to live up to an unattainable image cuts us off from our true needs and feelings. The danger to our well-being is that the fantasy person can become more real to us than who we really are. This real self, as Karen Horney defines it, is that "central inner force, common to all human beings and yet unique in each, which is the deep source of growth."

As we grow closer to our real self, we are also growing closer to our real values and goals in life. Yet many people maintain the illusion of their perfect self, and its extraordinary powers, at any physical or emotional cost. They will be a perfect mother, the most influential executive, the most respected editor, the most famous scientific researcher. . . .

"Lately," complains John, a salesman in the growing field of sports marketing, "I'm always exhausted. I feel hemmed in, my whole body cramped. Like you feel when you're jammed into a tiny seat on a crowded plane for a cross-country flight."

John is the top salesman in his company. He constantly drives himself to better a record that has already won him a fine salary, much praise, and many rewards. Not only is he exhausted, but success is clearly not making John very happy, and he is having family problems because of his excessive work schedule. His wife increasingly complains that he doesn't spend enough time with her and their children. Her criticism enrages him.

"I'm doing all this for them," he says, unable to keep from shouting. When asked about his extreme resentment over what is actually a positive idea—that his wife and children would like to see more of him—John only grows more irritated.

Hypersensitivity to criticism is perhaps the most common indication of the "tyranny of the shoulds." John is so driven by his false/perfect self that he concentrates only on what he fails to accomplish. Consequently, criticism, even in its mildest form, seems to support this failure and sounds to him like a harsh attack, an echo of his severe attacks on himself.

Although John concentrated his perfectionistic drives on business success, there are many variations. Other people will focus on being the perfect member of any relationship, the continually understanding parent, the inexhaustibly compassionate spouse, the unwaveringly generous friend.

Marion had great regrets over the failure of her relationship with her only sister, and blamed herself for not being more patient or understanding. Her very strict moral upbringing had made her feel it was sinful to speak negatively of anyone, especially a member of one's own family. In an early interview she said apologetically, "I shouldn't take her so seriously. I don't know what's wrong with me that I let her bother me so much."

Although she was worn down by her sister's constant criticisms and demands, Marion's sense of sin remained strong enough for her to continue taking responsibility for all the tension between them. She had never considered that her sister might be a difficult and mean-spirited person. Yet, from every indication in hearing about her, the sister seemed to be selfish and highly inconsiderate, and to have contributed very little to Marion's life. Even after Marion agreed that this might be a fair assessment of her sister, she was genuinely startled by the suggestion that we don't have to like people if they don't deserve liking, or continue to do all the work in a relationship, even one with an only sibling.

However, although it was hard at first, because of the tenacity of her early beliefs, as she continued to think about it

Marion found this new notion quite liberating. She still finds it painful not to be close to her sister, and feels bereft at the idea that closeness may never be possible, but she realizes she has to look elsewhere to find what she needs and wants in a relationship. She is concentrating on developing friendships with people who want the same sort of intimacy she does, and who reciprocate her ability to give.

The fact that there are times when we have to choose among certain relationships or competing experiences that we genuinely care about means there will always be some anguish in choice, especially when what we are giving up matters considerably.

Choosing can, and very often does, cause moral conflict, which will sometimes bring us considerable pain, says Martha Nussbaum, professor of philosophy at Brown University. She gives the common contemporary example of a parent who must decide whether to stay at work for an important meeting or go to a child's school play. Both are important, but since the parent cannot be in full control, or in two places at once, a difficult choice must be made.

The parent who understands that in choosing one, he or she neglects the other has made a painful decision, says Nussbaum, but is preferable, she implies, to the person who can simply dismiss or deny the dilemma of choice. The pain of choosing, she tells us, belongs to the passionate person who feels commitment and the ability to care deeply. To suffer the anguish of choice, Dr. Nussbaum believes, is to be fully human. *Regret can prompt us to clarify what we want from relationships.*

Georgia O'Keeffe's remarkable career presents another example of this profound human quandary. She left her ailing husband, the photographer Alfred Stieglitz, in New York City and settled in New Mexico for large parts of each year. She felt drawn to the southwestern terrain, which became a major source of inspiration for her painting.

The long separations were difficult for both Stieglitz and O'Keeffe, but were also essential to O'Keeffe's creative life. The marriage between these two artists was in many ways unconventional and therefore offered atypical amounts of personal freedom. But still, O'Keeffe, like all of us, had to wrestle with the recognition that the right choice for her might hurt someone she loved.

In another dilemma, although she is said to have loved and once wanted children, she never had any of her own. Looking back on her life in her ninety-eighth year, O'Keeffe admitted that her choices had not been without cost. She often felt, she said, as if she were walking a knife's edge: "On this knife, I might fall off on either side, but I'd walk it again."

When asked what would have happened if she had fallen off, she retorted sharply, "So what? So what if you do fall off? I'd rather be doing something I really want to do."

In midlife Georgia O'Keeffe was hospitalized for depression, which she apparently conquered by being truer to, and forgiving of, her own needs. She appears to have made peace with the idea that choosing always carries the risk of regret, and that only the real self can determine which risk is worth taking.

Work should not necessarily be the driving force of our lives, but O'Keeffe's life is a good example of how regret is transformed when the choices involved are made by being true to oneself. Clearly, fear of failure in her intimate relationships, or social disapproval, was less important to her than developing as an artist.

We continue to discover in an age of abundant choice that we can't have it all. However, the closer we grow to our real selves, the more likely we are to make choices that will help us develop our natural gifts and potential. And our goal should always be to make the most of this inherent potential, rather than to try to live up to an image of false perfection that can only breed disappointment and self-blaming regret.

Psychiatrist R. D. Laing confirmed that we are most truly guilty when we abandon "the obligation one owes to oneself." Yet a sense of personal inadequacy in comparison to other people, especially when measured against unreasonably high standards for ourselves, continues to breed the guilt that is so often attached to regret.

We often feel guilty when we think we've fallen short of our obligations to other people. At these times of assuming responsibility for offenses against someone else, we need to try realistically to assess our true culpability. An honest confrontation with our guilty feelings can help us decide, if we still feel at fault, what kinds of realistic reparations to make for these genuine regrets.

Lou has enrolled in college to pursue a degree after working for fifteen years as a drug and alcoholism counselor. He was raised in a ghetto area, and for many years worked in a rehabilitation program in a similar neighborhood, where he spent much of his time with hardened drug dealers. As he mingled on the college campus with younger students whose social attitudes were extremely liberal by comparison with his own, Lou was quite hostile and initially did his best to avoid any but necessary contact with his classmates. Gradually, however, he found himself growing to like and respect many of his fellow students, both black and white, and he began to realize that he carried some perceptions about young people, and young black people in particular, that were not only false but considerably biased. Recognizing Lou's struggle to adjust new impressions to deeply held beliefs, a sensitive professor about Lou's own age suggested he take a black studies course.

"The more I read novels and biographies of black people, the worse I felt about my own attitudes," Lou told us. "I couldn't believe how insensitive I had been to the struggles of so many people, and I had to admit that I had always been much harder on black people on the street than on most white people pulling the same crimes."

His professor helped Lou see that, considering his social background, it was hardly surprising that he had developed a number of *biases which his work life then easily reinforced.* This new perspective also helped Lou with his guilt over past abuses of official power. While he can't reconstruct the past, Lou is determined now to continue to grow into a more open, liberal person. He's added a number of philosophy courses to his program, and goes out of his way to continue his reading of ethnic writers so that he has a broader understanding of other people's histories. But he plans to do something much more concrete to make amends for past behavior.

"I'm going to try to get a job teaching in an elementary school. If I'm too old for a permanent appointment, I'll do as much substitute teaching as I can. I want to reach kids early, before they form these attitudes about how different they are from each other, and that being different from themselves is bad."

Reparation is one of the most effective ways to cope with the guilt we feel over real or imagined wrongdoing.

Confronting guilt feelings can also help us examine a possible pattern of assuming responsibility for what is truly *not* our fault. Either way, to make amends or to escape irrational self-blame, when guilty regret torments, we need to assess the feeling's validity and try to forgive ourselves for being merely human.

In his poem "A Dialogue of Self and Soul," William Butler Yeats describes the need to find compassion for our inescapable fallibility. They are words worth remembering in the struggle against regret:

> I am content to follow to its source
> Every event in action or in thought
> Measure the lot; forgive the lot!
> When such as I cast out remorse
> So great a sweetness flows into the breast . . .
> Everything we look upon is blest.

I feel that there has been some miscarriage, some wrong turning, but I do not know when it took place. . . .

—JOHN CHEEVER

THREE

Wrong Turns and Roads Not Taken

"Though we would like to live without regrets, and sometimes proudly insist that we have none," wrote James Baldwin, "this is not really possible, if only because we are mortal. . . . Between what one wishes to become, and what one has become, there can be a momentous gap. . . . And between the self as it is and the self as one sees it, there is also a distance, even harder to gauge." Many of us, he continues, feel "compelled to make a study of this baffling geography."

The geography of regret is baffling because it runs backward, full of wrong turns and roads not taken. The past stretches out behind us, and shadows of our former selves stand at each crossroads, reminding us that we once had a chance to choose different routes for our lives.

"It's been more than twenty years since I gave my baby up for adoption," said thirty-eight-year-old Tracy. "Every month that I don't conceive makes me more furious at my father for pushing me into that decision, and at myself even more for going along with it."

Tracy has recently completed her Ph.D. and is well established in a scientific career that she genuinely enjoys. She has been married for five years to another scientist a few years older than herself, and has been trying almost from the moment of their marriage to become pregnant. As she approaches forty her anxiety about conceiving is increasing.

Tracy was seventeen and looking forward to attending a prestigious college when she became pregnant. The boy, her first lover, quickly made it clear that he had no interest in fatherhood. Tracy was appalled at his callous attitude and felt both manipulated and frightened. She was enormously grateful when her parents took the news calmly and offered to help her.

Because of the family's religious beliefs, and also because abortion was illegal at the time, an abortion was out of the question. So Tracy went through with the pregnancy. However, it was her father's firm conviction that the baby should immediately be given up for adoption. For Tracy to attempt to raise a child as a teenage single parent would, he said firmly, not be good for the baby, and would ruin Tracy's obvious chances for a brilliant future.

Tracy was such an excellent student, and her parents so persuasive, that her high school granted permission for Tracy to leave school before the official end of her senior year. She was then sent to stay with a relative in an adjoining town, where her baby would be born during the summer. If all went well, Tracy would enter college on schedule in the fall.

"It all worked out very neatly, down to the last detail, which was typical of my father's way of doing business," Tracy says acidly. "At first I was happy to have him take charge. I was, understandably, feeling pretty overwhelmed. But then, as the pregnancy continued, I began to have second thoughts. I started to wonder whether I really wanted to give up my baby, and whether there wasn't a way to manage keeping it. Maybe I could put off college for a year, or go to a local college part-time, or even just find some way to convince my father to help me out financially."

Tracy had already begun adoption counseling with the agency that was arranging her baby's adoption, and she spoke to her counselor about her misgivings. "I felt she gave me no real support," Tracy says, these many years later still sounding intensely bitter. "Just like my father, she could only focus on my education and potential career, and she made me feel that my ideas about keeping the baby were completely unrealistic."

Since Tracy, at seventeen, had never made any major life decisions on her own before, she listened to the judgment of her parents and the counselor. However wistfully, she agreed that adoption was the only viable option. Afterward, she threw herself into school and managed to repress her regrets about giving up her child.

Over the years, however, society changed its attitudes toward such issues as single parenthood, and Tracy began to think that she might very well have managed to raise a child on her own. The idea that even when she had made her decision, she actually had more options than she realized fills her with anguish.

Although we link regret to choice, some regret is spawned by the illusion of having no choice.

For all of us, there are times in life when, because of a lack of information or experience, or the forcefulness of an authority figure whose judgment we feel we can't question, we accept the illusion of no choice. This can occur not just in one's personal life but in work situations as well. Without knowing we have other options, we can consider no alternative route, and so simply drift onto what seems the only possible path or go where we've been directed.

Tracy's regret is now greatly intensified by feeling that she could have tried harder to keep her child. Particularly as she remains unable to conceive again, she torments herself with accusations of being blind to, or not being assertive enough to insist on, this alternative option.

A lack of assertiveness is a primary source of many contemporary regrets.

Although so many people do list this issue as a major

regret, the term *assertiveness* is often misused in modern society. It is filled with competitive and aggressive implications that can have quite negative effects on our lives. If we are supposed to conquer every obstacle, never give in, always win out, our self-esteem will always be in jeopardy. For if success is the inevitable result of drive and superior ability, then any failure or disappointment is destined to be seen as painful proof of some personal deficiency. Seen by whom? By ourselves, of course—our harshest critics.

Compassion for our missteps becomes impossible as we engage in punishing second-guessing. "If only," "Why didn't I?" "I could have," "I should have" become the language of senseless and unproductive self-blame. Rejecting the idea that everyone (even the most perfect person) has limitations, we engage in what Freud called "turning against oneself," looking at ourselves with hostility and disdain for having failed to do the impossible. Furthermore, if winning is all that matters, we will too often find our choices influenced by values that have painfully little to do with our own deepest convictions.

On the other hand, real assertiveness has little to do with winning or competition or power. When making choices, real assertiveness involves defining what we truly want from life and starting out to find it, no matter what other people think of our decision and direction.

Such self-assertion is connected to the *constructive use of regret, because knowing what we regret about life so far can motivate us to demand something better in the future.* Too often, though, intead of using regret as a measure of what is lacking and what needs changing, we remain mired unproductively in the past.

"There was a woman in graduate school whom I had an enormous crush on," says Gary, twice divorced. "But I was certain she'd never look at me. It's fifteen years later, and I've never met anyone as interesting as she was. Maybe it's because every other relationship has failed that I keep thinking that she might actually have been responsive, if I'd had the guts to pursue a relationship with her. I can't stop kicking myself for not even trying."

Gary's self-denigration at being "such a wimp" is a misuse of the positive potential of regret. Obviously, it isn't useful to spend so much time regretting a relationship that never was, unless he is ready to try actively to find the woman and see if a relationship is still possible. Gary would be much better off if he could address his current problems about intimacy and try to figure out why he is allowing himself to waste new opportunities for finding love and fulfillment.

Writer Jane Smiley *was* able to return to the past and actively reexamine a "might-have-been." Following her divorce, she deliberately sought out a man she had formerly loved. After they had probed their old problems from a more mature perspective, anger and disappointment gave way to the mutual realization that they had "made plenty of mistakes—separately but also together."

This recognition helped soften their regret over once losing each other, and within a short time of their reunion, they married. The marriage, with its rich blend of past and present experience, seems, says Ms. Smiley, wonderfully "old and new all at once."

Not everyone has the ability or opportunity to begin again or even to make things better the second time around. Greater pain appears, however, in those who never began at all. *All* of our research confirms that we regret the things we didn't do more than any of the things we may have mistakenly done.

The road not taken causes far more suffering than a wrong turn.

According to a University of Arizona study on priorities and regrets, for example, one of the most common regrets felt by both men and women is that they did not pursue more education, or work harder while they were in school. Looking at what they judge to be their meager accomplishments, they ask themselves a haunting question: "Who knows what we might have become had we tried to be more?" This is a question that applies to every aspect of experience, from traveling to new places, to developing natural talents, to building strong intimate relationships.

"I'm not so unhappy at my life being over," said a terminally ill man we spoke to. "I'm unhappy because I have never lived." We don't have to be faced with serious illness to know the particularly poignant regret of the unlived life. Indeed, success along the road we do take can't be counted on to diminish a longing for the road not taken.

When writer, congresswoman, and ambassador Clare Boothe Luce died, her obituary noted: "She had enough careers to satisfy the ambitions of several women." Yet, in an interview not long before her death, Mrs. Luce said, "If I were to write an autobiography, my title would be *The Autobiography of a Failure.*"

She explained her surprising judgment of her life this way: "Failure means you haven't done your best with the talents or opportunities you were given. . . . My failure was not to return to the real vocation I had, which was writing [for the theater]."

When her husband, Henry Luce, the publisher of *Time* magazine (who was contemptuous of the theater, calling it "night work"), urged her to give up writing and run for Congress, she listened to his judgment and to that of others and, indeed, was elected to two congressional terms. However, she never found satisfaction in the political arena because, to her mind, "it isn't a personal, creative effort." So, although Mrs. Luce was celebrated and envied by others, she found her life terribly wanting. In turning from writing, she lost touch with her own real values and needs.

Our best tool in avoiding wrong turns or passing by roads that we really should take, is to try to make choices that are based on true personal values. Then, no matter how disappointed we are if we fail to reach our goals, we will have less regret for the decision to pursue them, and more compassion than self-blame for our failures.

"I think about the last six years and all the things I could have done differently." Mike sums up his story with a rueful smile. "But I was raised to believe in the sanctity of marriage, and I still believe it, even now. So, I kept trying to make things work out for Jill and me, even to the point of agreeing to move out of the house so she could 'have some time alone to think things over.'

"It was a real financial handicap, keeping up two places those eight months, and I saw my kids less, which I hated. It was only when Jill continued to refuse any marriage counseling, or in any way to try to solve our problems, that I realized she had never intended anything to come of our separation except the freedom to live by herself and not have to pay any rent."

Mike's willingness to go along with his wife's demands created many regrets for him, but even if he feels foolish for being naïve, he is comfortable with the thought that he made mistakes only because he hoped to save his marriage. For him, marriage and family were so important that he was willing to try anything to save them. Mike knew what he needed, and chose to do everything he could to satisfy those needs.

Some people, including even his ex-wife, may see him as passive, pushed around and taken advantage of, but that doesn't shake Mike's conviction that his choices were real choices after all. They sprang from his deepest personal beliefs. It would not have been "like Mike" to give up any sooner.

On the other hand, Mike has learned something important from the very unhappy experience. The regret he feels over his divorce has helped him to understand that maintaining a relationship should not take superhuman powers. As he puts it, "I'll never again get into a situation where I feel like a failure because I can't *make* someone love me."

Knowing what our true values are also helps us determine whether we are ready to risk new experiences. This is an age-old dilemma, found even in the classic mythological motif, the hero's journey. As Joseph Campbell explains the myth, it mirrors the "transformation" we all have to go through as we relinquish the protection we found in dependency, and move out to the alarmingly unfamiliar, unprotected, and challenging terrain of mature, responsible, autonomous life.

While we may not feel heroic as we stand at some modern threshold, wanting to move, to change, to quit, to leave, we are actually attempting our own kinds of psychological transformation. Often we take one step forward and then stop, barraged by paralyzing and endless *what ifs*. What if we fail? What if we can't handle what lies ahead? What if we give up what we have, only to end up worse off than before? Alarming as these questions are, we need to try to find the courage to face the risk of failure. For, as Erich Fromm also says about the heroic impulse, "Heroes are those with the courage to leave what they have . . . and move out, not without fear, but without succumbing to their fear."

People who are least satisfied with the way their lives have turned out wish that they had "taken more risks."

When safety is chosen over risk, the journey we decided on can come to seem boring and alarmingly pointless. The road we have selected is disappointing, depressing, and, in terms of wasted opportunity, dismaying.

"My husband wanted to take our wedding presents and savings and take a year off and go to Europe when we married," says Diane, a suburban housewife with three small children. She looks around her traditionally decorated living room, and grimaces. "This isn't really the way I wanted to live. . . . It's how I was afraid not to live. We would have had to budget very carefully if we'd gone off to Europe, probably have had to take odd jobs to stay all that time . . . and neither of us spoke any other languages. I don't know. It all just seemed scary to me. And the truth is, I was also just afraid of doing something so unconventional. Now, my husband is deeply into a career. We've got these kids. . . . I'll be an old lady before I'll ever have the freedom again for such an extended trip, and what good will it do me then?"

Diane mourns a missed adventure at a time of life when adventure was truly possible. Greg, a hospital administrator, regrets that he backed away from an intellectual challenge that might have led to a more distinguished career. Sacrificing a chance at growth for the safety of limited goals seems small comfort in safety's aftermath, although Greg's ambivalence is understandable. As Erich Fromm explained, "not to move forward . . . is very tempting. We fear, and consequently avoid, taking a step into the unknown, the uncertain . . . for before we take that step the new aspects beyond it appear very risky, and hence frightening."

"I applied to medical school to please my father," Greg tells us, "but I never for a minute thought I would be accepted, and in fact the only school that did take me on was some relatively minor university in the Southwest. My father talked himself blue trying to convince me that I would be able to handle the work there, but I was certain I couldn't. School was always a chore for me, and I simply thought I'd rather not go at all than deal with the shame of flunking out. And I guess I would have to say I was also trying to rebel against my father's authority, even though I really knew he had my best interests at heart.

"At first I thought I was making a pretty good compromise by going into hospital administration. But now that I'm well into my thirties, I'm feeling worse and worse. I see these young doctors every day, and I know they're no brighter than I was at their age. I hate myself for giving up before I even began. It seems to me that because of some awful mix of fear and adolescent defiance, I've become an administrative hack who's completely wasted my intellectual potential."

While *risk* is clearly a subjective term, ranging from learning to swim to overcoming a fear of flying, from reaching beyond our limits to substituting adventure for convention, or revealing personal feelings, many of us hesitate to replace the familiar with even the most exciting unknown possibility. The fact that we want both safety and satisfaction in life means it takes enormous courage to risk losing safety to gain satisfaction when the two goals—as so often happens—don't coalesce.

However, when we do face apprehension with courage, even a failed attempt to get something we really wanted can still make us feel better about ourselves.

"Rob and I were best buddies at work," said Lauren, a most attractive woman of forty-one. "We're both married, and our mates are both lawyers, and yet neither of us ever made any move toward expanding the friendship into a foursome. We were strictly an exclusive weekday relationship.

"About a year ago, I found myself almost obsessing about Rob, replaying in my head our wonderfully funny conversations at lunch or the occasional late workday dinner. Then I began to have sexual dreams, and I'd catch him looking at me in a way that suddenly made me feel sure he was experiencing the same changed—and charged—feelings toward me. Good Lord." She sighed, throwing up her hands. "What can I tell you? . . . I just convinced myself we were in love with each other but were both afraid to admit it.

"So, about three months ago, we were out of town on an assignment, and I decided this was it. I wasn't going to wait for him to make the first move. I lured him up to my room with the promise of some hundred-year-old brandy that I had quite deliberately packed in my bag. And as we sat there drinking and talking in the marvelously companionable way that was so special between us, I reached out and touched his face, and told him that I'd realized my feelings for him had changed from friendship to something much more passionate.

"I thought the poor man was going to burn with embarrassment. The flush on his cheeks was definitely not from the brandy. But once I had gotten started, I couldn't stop. . . . I refused to see how he was responding—or, to be more accurate, not responding," she finished with a giggle.

Behind Lauren's attempt at lighthearted self-mockery there is obvious pain that a deeply sustaining friendship has come to an end. "We speak, but only in the most superficial way now . . . and we haven't had a meal alone together since the night of my declaration. But I don't regret the experience.

"To begin with," she carefully explained, "I'm really a rather timid person. I like to play it safe, not stir things up. This was the first time in my entire life that I ever stuck my neck out for something I wasn't sure in advance would work out. I'm pleased about that.

"Secondly, I would have gone on fantasizing forever about Rob if this hadn't happened. And I just decided that whatever regret I feel that I'd read him wrong isn't as bad as the regret I might have when I was sixty or seventy and looking back on my life and wondering what course my life might have taken if I had been brave enough to speak up. I truly believe now that the biggest risk of all may be not ever risking.

"Finally, and maybe this is the most important result of the experience, the intensity of my regret over Rob's rebuff forced me to take another look at my marriage. Obviously, if I was really satisfied *there,* I wouldn't have been so susceptible to him. I'm in therapy now and so is my husband, and we're working at making the marriage more vital. I also believe, though, that because I was able to cope with the risk of opening up to Rob, if the relationship with my husband doesn't improve, I'll have the courage to face the next step of considering life on my own."

Lauren took the risk of looking foolish for expressing her real feelings and possibly being rejected by a person she cared about. In a way, May took an ever greater risk when she moved beyond her fear of rejection and even ridicule by a large group of people: the academic community in which she had previously found her self-definition.

May is a professor at a fine private college and the author of a much-praised, if turgid, treatise on political theory. Last spring (just before her thirty-fifth birthday) she turned down a guest professorship at an ivy league university to take a sabbatical and enroll in an intensive creative writing course.

It was a season of remarkable contentment, and one that

changed her life. While she is back to teaching now, her future is filled with new, exhilarating options.

"My parents really pushed me into academia. I'm the first child in my family to go to graduate school, and one of only a few who went to college. I was smart and got scholarships and I suppose I felt I had no choice but to take advantage of my opportunities. I never really thought about other choices, especially when I'd started becoming successful and fully playing the part of the clever young professor with a glowing academic road stretched out ahead of her.

"My book won prizes, but I wouldn't read it if I hadn't written it," she says with a wide grin. "It's plain and simply *boring*, unless you happen to be vitally interested in this tiny corner of research. And writing it was also completely joyless. All the time I was hunched over my notes, I was worrying about how my more prestigious colleagues were going to evaluate the book, and so, of course, how they would evaluate me as a legitimate peer.

"Now that I've explored writing fiction—whether I decide to leave teaching or not—the big breakthrough is simply viewing myself as a writer, not only as a scholar. Somebody who can write what she wants to and tries to communicate with a general audience rather than worrying about criticism from two hundred 'important' people. Sure, my book had some value, but I only wrote it to prove myself to the scholarly community. Not anymore. It's so liberating!

"It's really amazing," she says softly. "I knew, deep inside, as soon as I started to write my first short story, that no matter how it turned out, in terms of my making a living as a writer, what I was doing was going to help me avoid a major, powerful regret down the road . . . the realization that I had never been true to myself. I'm not saying I know who that self is yet," she says quickly. "But I sure know I'll never find out if I go on *pretending* to be someone just to please someone else."

As happened with Ambassador Luce, May's regret over what was lacking in her life allowed her to realize that success can be empty even if it generates the envy and approval of others. It was not easy to drop the definition of herself as a scholar and its accompanying cultural approval, but she was brave enough to admit that no matter how much other people envied or admired her, they were not seeing the May she truly was or wanted to be.

The psychologist Abraham Maslow, who understood the difficulties in allowing the true inner self to emerge, warned that our "inner nature is not strong and overpowering and unmistakable like the instincts of animals. It is weak and delicate and subtle and easily overcome by habit, cultural pressure, and wrong attitudes toward it."

While every day this warning seems more apt as the voices encouraging "wrong attitudes" grow louder, May discovered that dropping the pretenses that muffled her genuine voice was far less of a risk, or a sacrifice, than she'd been led to imagine. A scholar still, she smilingly quoted William James to sum up her new attitude about life: "To give up pretensions is as blessed a relief as to have them gratified!"

Still, the fact that we do seek both security and pleasure in life means we will frequently feel considerable stress when we sacrifice security in pleasure's pursuit. It will help us tolerate the tension to remember that not all stress is harmful. Hans Selye, the father of stress research, identified "eustress" (adapted from the science of eugenics) as the kind of stress which helps us grow despite any temporary discomfort from our tension.

Regret can be a form of eustress. Indeed, it can be argued that *the worse regret makes us feel, the greater our possibility for growth*. Regret, as it intensifies, can push us finally to confront the false values and illusions that led to our present self-blame and distress.

Perhaps the most troublesome illusions have to do with our longing for love. Just as we grow up with idealized images of the kinds of people we should become, we tend to idealize our lovers: **"If this special person loves me, I must be all right."**

As we layer illusion after illusion on a lover, covering over all flaws and failings, it becomes increasingly difficult either to sustain a relationship in the real world or to let go—and not to be overcome by self-reproach—when, despite our resistance, the relationship ends. Idealization of a lover leaves us haunted by the conviction that we were not good enough to make the relationship work.

Janine's self-blame and depression over a broken love affair had her clinging to the familiar rituals of the obsessed. She stayed home every night in case he might call to apologize for leaving. She opened her mailbox after work with a pounding heart, hoping to see a familiar hand. The letter she imagined receiving would forgive her for what she had done wrong, for she was convinced that the breakup was her fault.

When Janine talked about Bob, it was always in completely idealized terms. She could see his adventurousness but never his insensitivity. She believed the values he preached about love but had clearly tuned out what had been obvious examples of his own frail commitment. She wept over his remembered passion for her, and refused the suggestion that he had always had a weakness for other women. The fact that he had actually left her for another woman only made her feel more deficient.

For a long and painful time Janine was truly incapable of seeing the situation as it really was. She only grew angry when friends told her she was painting a picture of a man who had never really existed. Had she been able to see Bob's weaknesses as well as her own, Janine could have moved ahead with her life, but because she idealized him she could only look backward for the joy she had found and lost and was certain she would never find again.

Janine had never allowed herself to question the authenticity of her lover's character or the depth of his feelings, for to do so would have punctured her fragile sense of well-being. Everyone wants to be loved and approved of, and most of us want to find a steady, supportive life partner. But when, like Janine, we feel worthwhile only if someone else cares about us, we don't just want love, we believe we *need* love to survive emotionally. With one wrenching goodbye, that man or woman whose love makes us whole can leave us feeling desperately inadequate and incomplete. As Erich Fromm wrote: "If I am what I have and if what I have is lost, who then am I?"

Though most of us do have a tendency to idealize personal relationships, we can also do the same to people in our professional lives, like a boss or co-worker or mentor. Perhaps even more important, we can idealize lost opportunities. While we inevitably feel wistful about any chance of happiness that slipped away, we can become convinced that the lost opportunity was the only one that mattered.

"I turned down an acting role," says an actress named Catherine, "because my agent didn't share my enthusiasm for the project. I'm very much in awe of him because he has some very well-known clients, and I guess I don't feel as important as they are, so I'm always concerned about his approval. Anyway, I turned the role down, and then I learned that a colleague of mine had taken the part on for a really big salary.

"I simply couldn't stop thinking about what I'd given up. I was so angry at myself for not going with my intuition, and for not being stronger about insisting that I wanted to do the play—which, of course, I was certain would turn out to be a smash hit. I don't consider myself an envious person, but I kept coming up with these fantasies about how much money it was going to earn, and how famous it was going to make the other actress!"

Fortunately, early on, Catherine was able to observe herself getting tangled in the web of self-reproach, and took some steps to turn her regret into something productive. "I told myself that despite my certainty that I had passed up a once-in-a-lifetime chance for fame and fortune, nobody really knows what play is going to do well—audiences' tastes are too whimsical for that. And, while I still regret not standing up to my agent and not listening to myself rather than to him, instead of blaming myself I'm trying to fire up the energy to find a role I can really get excited about, even if it's in regional theater rather than on Broadway. I've spent too much time trying to get the professionally 'smart' jobs. Now I'm determined to make developing as an actress my real priority."

Finally and purposefully gaining control of our idealized fantasies about "the one that got away" brings a wonderful new sense of freedom. Reality takes hold, and we are able to see that our life isn't over because of one loss and that we can learn from, rather than only blame ourselves for, even major mistakes.

Regret is, in many ways, the key to living realistically and authentically. If we aren't able to accept our mistakes, we can't learn from them. We would always be like small children, sweetly innocent of experience. Unsullied, yes; optimistic, perhaps; but wise? No. And it is the wisdom of experience that carries us through life. Accepting and taking responsibility for our experience will help us to hear the spontaneous voice of—and take direction from—our real selves. Poet May Sarton describes the joy of such self-discovery and acceptance:

> All fuses now, falls into place
> From wish to action, word to silence,
> My work, my loves, my time, my face
> Gathered into one intense
> Gesture of growing like a plant.

And the point is to live everything
Live the questions now
Perhaps you will gradually without noticing it
Live along some distant day into the answers.

—RAINER MARIA RILKE

FOUR

Self-Deception and Regret

There is a large and complex system of psychological defenses that we use to avoid the anxiety of troublesome questions. We also—often automatically—call up these defenses when faced with circumstances that are more than we feel emotionally able to handle. As we will see in a later chapter, some defenses do help us adjust to, and cope better with, difficult situations. However, some other defenses are not reliable tools for coping, as they don't really help us resolve the problem. Instead, they reinforce denial of the problem's existence, as well as of our genuine feelings.

People have always been tempted to use their capacity for denial, but modern life intensifies the temptation. Because we live in a culture of copious choice, and regret is so connected to the anxieties of choice, we can, without even realizing it, form a simple equation: *If we deny any doubts about our decisions, then we can escape the regret that appears in doubt's path.*

There are many ways to describe the differences between our defenses. Some psychologists will call them upper and lower level, or mature and immature, or primitive and sophisticated. We will simply refer to them as being more or less effective in helping us cope with emotional stress and, in particular, with the sorrowful stress of regret.

Less-effective defenses all involve not admitting our true feelings into awareness, in ways that are eventually unproductive. It can be tempting to use these lesser defenses, for they do momentarily push troublesome feelings underground. However, buried feelings are also feelings that go unexplored, and only in understanding our true feelings can we ever hope to deal with them constructively.

In our attempts to make ourselves more comfortable, we can distort reality so that we aren't equipped to meet reality's demands.

Denial is one of the most frequently used of the less-effective defenses, particularly as a response to regret. In its most drastic form, denial is a flat refusal to admit that anything is wrong. We either perceive reality as we need to see it—not as it actually is—or we insulate ourselves from understanding the reality of a situation by denying the evidence at hand. Psychoanalyst Reuven Bar-Levav offers an extremely tragic example of this process. "Many intelligent and knowledgeable Jews . . . paid very dearly for denying the danger of Hitler's rise to power," he explains, for "this is often how we react to extreme fear."

The impulse to make reality more palatable did indeed prevent many German Jews from recognizing that they needed to flee their homeland before the impending Holocaust, and this remains a profound regret for many survivors whose families were destroyed by the Nazis. Their denial obviously was in every possible way unproductive. For, while "in the short run," says Dr. Bar-Levav, denial "helps in warding off painful and frightening realizations, the ability to cope with reality remains grossly impaired. The eventual awakening, which cannot be postponed forever, is always more rude and more painful than it would have been otherwise."

On a different scale, consider the family who hears the painful news that the father, the principal breadwinner, has lost his job. Denying the threat to their way of life can temporarily help them all to absorb the initial shock, but their denial is ultimately not effective. If the family continues to resist an honest assessment of the situation, they won't be able to deal with their problems realistically. The father will not mobilize himself to meet the stress of job-hunting and its frequent blows to self-esteem, and his family may not make the necessary life-style adjustments, such as reducing expenses until their income is replaced. Or, if the stress of looking for work finally forces the father to face reality, the family's continuing denial will isolate him from them, robbing him of the support he needs to face his daily ordeal, and not offering him comfort for his frustration and fears.

If we often deny immediate life-threatening or pride-shattering situations, we also deny regrets from the past, in a complex attempt to ward off similar pain in the future.

"I've lived my life just fine, thank you," Nora announced at our first meeting, when we asked about the long-term effects of her totally deprived childhood. "I got no support from my family in any way, and that's been all right with me. I never have, and I never will waste my time regretting what I didn't get from them."

A tall, imposing woman with a dramatic flair, Nora is very proud of her rise from emotionally impoverished beginnings. She owns a successful clothing boutique with a clientele, she quickly tells us, that is very important and affluent. "I get plenty of admiration from my customers," she says with a brilliant smile. "It more than makes up for the criticism and coldness I always got from my parents."

In a second visit with Nora, which took place several months later, her demeanor was more subdued. She told us that her long estrangement from her parents had been broken when she learned that her father was dying. In the last few weeks of his life Nora spent considerable time at the hospital with her mother.

"We started to talk and I began to think that my mother was actually a victim, too, of her own really very harsh upbringing. In any case, maybe because her attention was so focused on my father, she wasn't so critical of me. She didn't even carry on about my staying away for so long. She just really seemed happy to have me there now.

"I started to feel differently toward her, but every time I left the hospital, I'd close right up again. I wasn't going to let myself be taken in by her, just because she was acting a little warmer. I knew it wouldn't last."

Impulsively, although her father was so ill, Nora decided to take a business trip. She flew to several European cities and made some remarkable buying coups. When she returned home two weeks later her father was still hospitalized, and while her mother didn't directly comment on Nora's absence, she once again acted aloof.

"I knew she was furious that I had left her alone, but I wasn't about to apologize to her. I don't owe her anything, and I don't need to win her approval any more now than I ever did."

Even though Nora kept referring to the trip's success and tried to sound as definite and self-assured as she usually did, she seemed more sad than angry. We asked her then whether she felt something might have changed in her relationship with her mother if she hadn't gone away on business but had continued to share the family vigil. While Nora insisted that the question was irrelevant, that it didn't matter to her what her mother thought, it was clear from her extreme defensiveness and obvious dejection that she did regret severing the tentative connection she had begun to make with her mother.

It's probably safe to say that one of the reasons Nora took the trip was to flee the discomfort she felt at the surfacing of buried regrets about their relationship. Had Nora been able to admit these feelings, she might not have taken the trip at all, or she would at least have been able to discuss her mother's feelings about it when she returned. She might have allowed herself to see that in the name of self-sufficiency she was denying deep hurt and emotional need, and she might have found the courage and strength to reach out for parental love once more. Nora's need to pull back instead of reaching out is an illustration of someone protecting herself from future hurt by denying, and therefore never attempting to resolve, the powerful emotions still evoked by a source of past pain.

Repression is another way we push painful thoughts and feelings from our consciousness. We automatically "forget" traumatic experiences and memories that are too painful to remember. A quintessential example of repression is the incest victim who very often "forgets" her early abuse. Boston psychiatrist Judith Herman studied a group of incest victims and concluded that repressing the experiences was the only way they could have survived their horror. "They had memory gaps for good reasons," says Dr. Herman. Indeed, she found that those women with the most "severe amnesia" were the ones who had suffered the most "violent, sadistic abuse."

Incest victims often find their first confrontations with what really happened to them in dreams and nightmares. Because repressed memories do slip past barriers into our dreams, for all of us the dream is frequently a key to all sorts of hidden, hurtful feelings. Little glimpses of the past invade the night until they begin to form a full picture that can—if we allow it—provide the opportunity for daytime recognition of some buried or even current problems.

Sylvia is the mother of three children. She prides herself on her successful mothering. Despite comments from teachers and concerned family members that her middle child, a pensive, rather fragile boy, seemed troubled, she denied that he was any less happy than his brother and sister.

Eventually, however, she was coerced by her husband to take the boy to family counseling. During the course of treatment, she had a dream that her son was sitting on the edge of a riverbank while the rest of the family frolicked in the water. As Sylvia recounted the dream scene, she burst into tears. "He seemed so lonely," she said. "There we all were, boating and swimming and water-skiing . . . and he was just sitting there, staring at us, as if he didn't have any part in our lives at all."

With the help of her therapist, Sylvia realized after this dream that because she so deeply regretted the quality of her relationship with her middle child and, on some deep level, felt that she had contributed to his sadness, she needed to deny that the boy was unhappy. Sylvia had used repression to avoid seeing the truth of her son's experience, and in so doing had rejected his own deepest needs.

Even without a therapist, it is possible to examine our dreams for their messages from the dreamer to the wakeful self. Thomas Wolfe spoke of the "telescopic magic of a dream," and indeed we can use our dreams to peer into all the corners of our lives. If we wake up feeling tense, it's useful to try to remember our dream stories and symbols and see if they relate to any current challenges or problems. Often, in this way, dreams can help us identify regrets that we've repressed because they seemed too painful to face, thereby helping us finally to confront the regrets so that we can work on resolving them on a conscious level.

Turning against the self is a defense we use especially to protect ourselves from feeling anger toward someone who is the real source of our stress. This could be an employer who holds enough power over our lives that expressing anger might create professional risk; a parent, mate, lover, or close friend whose love and approval we don't dare lose; or a child toward whom acknowledging anger would make us feel horrendously guilty. Instead of feeling the anger or frustration toward this troublesome other, we turn the feelings inward and rage against ourselves, frequently falling into depression and a shameful sense of inadequacy.

When our regrets are linked to other people toward whom we feel but can't admit anger, we can hold ourselves completely responsible for what went wrong in a relationship, or for what is missing from our lives.

Emily is a devoted mother to a teenage child who has always suffered from rheumatoid arthritis. Although Peter has made considerable progress over the years, he continues to have flare-ups that require a great deal of care, and Emily's life has been severely constrained by the demands his condition makes on her time.

As Peter matured, Emily's husband and many of her friends encouraged her to try to get the boy to be more independent. They feel that Peter is capable of doing much more for himself than he seems willing to do, and that his demands on his mother are unreasonable and excessive.

"But how could I say no to that poor boy who's suffered so much?" Emily explained her earlier attitude toward her son. "All I wanted was that he find some happiness in life, and to try to make up for his handicap." Clearly, Peter's struggles and periods of genuinely severe discomfort blocked Emily from facing—let alone ever expressing—even the smallest degree of resentment or anger toward him.

"I was always so frustrated," she recalled. "But never with him, only myself! I felt there was absolutely nothing I could do right to make him happy, that my life as his mother was just one long failure, and yet there was nothing else I could be or do with my life, considering the extent of his needs. I'd get so frustrated at what seemed his perpetual glumness, having him frown instead of smile when I'd do something I thought was special, like bringing home a movie on videotape because he wasn't well enough to go out to see one in a theater. Invariably, what I chose would be a picture he didn't really want to see. It wasn't that he was hostile or even complaining," Emily hastened to assure us, almost reflexively making sure we didn't think badly of her son. "He'd just look disappointed or sad, and I'd blame myself for only reminding him of his restrictions by trying to compensate for them in this way. Finally, I was feeling so helpless and depressed at the whole situation that my husband insisted I get some counseling."

Emily shook her head and smiled at the memory of that first therapeutic visit.

"After I told the counselor my story he just looked at me for a couple of minutes, and then he asked, 'Don't you know tyranny when you see it? Don't you see how angry you are at your son's control of your life?'

"My first response was to be flooded with panic at the idea that I might be angry with Peter. I know it sounds ridiculous, but until that moment I had never seen that I had legitimate reason to be resentful of him even though I loved him. I knew I was frustrated and always mad at myself for not being able to manage things better, but I never ever felt any anger toward my son."

Being able to acknowledge the real source of her depression freed Emily to deal constructively with her anger. For one thing, she was able to ward some of it off by ceasing to be so subservient to Peter's often unreasonable demands. Not feeling so guilty about her repressed feelings allowed her to see that much of her response to Peter was primarily based on avoiding guilt, rather than on what was truly in his best interest. She was able then to work on not feeling guilty about setting limits or failing to make him always satisfied or happy. "For the first time since his condition was diagnosed, I think, I have begun to truly take pleasure in our relationship," she says, "and I know it's because for the first time I've really accepted the relationship's problems and limitations."

Emily will always deeply regret that Peter has to live with a life-constricting handicap, and to some degree her heartache will always complicate her feelings for her son. As Rollo May notes, parents of a troubled child often find that their regrets are bound up in resentment at the child for causing them "such perplexity and suffering." To conquer the resentment truly, he affirms, we have to liberate ourselves through compassion not only for the child's problems but for our own parental response to their struggles. "Compassion . . ." says May, "helps us judge less harshly ourselves as well as the persons who impinge upon us."

Intellectualization is another protective, but ultimately hazardous, defense. The stereotypes of the detached scientist and aloof academic who can be supremely rational and intellectually aware, but who don't really know what they're feeling, are good examples of people who approach experience with too much rational detachment. When we intellectualize our regrets, we don't try to deny the experience itself, but rather the painful feelings the experience may arouse.

There are clearly times when some degree of intellectualization can help us adapt to difficult situations. For example, a surgeon may protect himself from the tension of a serious operation by approaching the task on a largely intellectual level, detaching himself from his feelings about the risks involved. However, if he relies on this defense too much, while he may still be technically effective, he can be emotionally unavailable to patients and their families during a time when they are deeply needy, and also may become increasingly out of touch with his feelings even in his private life.

Intellectualizing regrets in personal relationships too often blocks us from realizing our true feelings, and consequently from dealing with a serious interpersonal problem. "It didn't bother me that my wife was having an affair," Ned insisted. "I figured if she needed to do that, it was her dilemma. I really don't regret not making it more of an issue in our marriage. I never felt that it was my fault that she was looking elsewhere because I wasn't satisfying her, or anything like that. I always believed it was just some basically neurotic need of hers, perhaps a fear of getting old . . . looking for assurance that she was still attractive. I've read a great deal about those sorts of motivating factors in infidelity. So I stayed with her and chose not to make a big deal out of it."

Two years after his wife's affair began, she told Ned she

wanted a divorce. The only feeling he recalls about his reaction to the news was surprise. In answer to our questions he continued to keep his feelings at bay, preferring to offer detailed statistics about changing cultural patterns of infidelity, and how often casual affairs develop in intensity and eventually cause divorce.

During several interviews with Ned, his disengagement was as insulating as if we were separated by a high wall. He confesses to being lonely, but five years after his divorce he has not yet formed any real attachment to another woman.

When Ned insists that he has no regrets about his life, he is not convincing. His underlying discouragement and fears of intimacy are not hard to spot. The cool appraisal of his personal experience is protecting him from immediate emotional pain, but unfortunately, it also suggests that he will continue to be as emotionally bereft as he is today.

Rationalization is a companion defense to intellectualization, and the two frequently occur together. Rationalization is especially pertinent to regret, for by coming up with a set of legitimate reasons for our irrational actions and choices, we never have to admit that we may have made a mistake. We try to accept our own invented version of the truth, fervently offering it up to ourselves and anyone else who seems to suggest that our behavior may have been misguided. For example: we never really wanted the career we gave up when we married . . . we can't take the job offer across the country because our parents would miss us too much . . . we have to keep drinking because it helps us to relax . . . our children don't mind us working such long hours, because they're learning how to be independent.

A common method of rationalizing is to blame someone else for our mistakes or dissatisfactions. "I don't have fun anymore, because he doesn't like to do anything!" Doris complains of her husband, to whom she has been married for ten years. "He'll never go to the theater, hardly ever even a movie or out for dinner at a really nice restaurant, and God knows we never go anyplace like a nightclub, even though I absolutely love to dance. So I have absolutely no social life. How I wish I had married someone who wanted to enjoy life instead of just sitting the whole experience out!"

Through counseling, Doris was eventually able to see that accusing her husband was a cover for her own anxiety. While her husband's lack of energy and enthusiasm was certainly cramping her social life, what she really regretted was her own—never resolved—dependency. Blaming him for her boredom was an attempt to stave off the much larger regret of never taking responsibility for her own needs, or for failing to become a more autonomous person.

Circumstances, not just people, can also be blamed for our mistakes. Rationalization serves as a reasonable excuse for behavior that might otherwise engender considerable regret.

Victor came to our interview carrying his sleeping infant son in a carry-sack. Laying the child down in a quiet corner, he kept looking over at him as we talked.

Victor is one of the growing number of men who have started second families in midlife. His paternal joy is sincere, and very engaging, but when we asked about the grown children from his former marriage, the atmosphere abruptly changed. Victor was immediately defensive.

"Well, we're not very close. I know they resent that I'm so tied up with my new family, but they don't understand! How could I have given them the same kind of attention when they were small? I was just starting out, and I hardly earned anything. Sure, I worked too long, and wasn't around very much for them, but I had no choice!"

If Victor seemed always ready to reach out and embrace his new baby, he clearly also wanted to hold regret over his older children at arm's length. To admit regret would have been to face an anxiety-producing truth about his life. The missed relationships with his older children reflect choices he made about priorities, and can't be totally passed off to circumstance. A constructive use of regret in this situation would have been to admit some responsibility for his other children's estrangement. Painful as the admission might be, it could have led Victor to make some effort toward reclaiming those initial father-child connections.

While denial is an extreme defense against admitting regret, paradoxically, being totally mired in regret can also be a defensive strategy. *Unyielding regret can be a way of escaping responsibility for decisive action.*

"There is that might-have-been which is the single rock we cling to above the maelstrom of unbearable reality," wrote William Faulkner. It may seem strange to think that persistent regret over what might have been can be an attempt to ease the pain of what is, but many people try to use regret—consciously or unconsciously—in exactly this way.

Evelyn is the fifty-year-old unmarried daughter of an emotionally dependent, long-widowed mother. At night, sitting in her shadowed living room after her mother went to sleep, Evelyn would drift into lost dreams, savoring remembered moments of passion and grieving over unfulfilled promises from lovers she had long since renounced. As the years went by, regret over not having married became the principal theme of Evelyn's life. Although she was and is an attractive woman, she made no effort to meet men, joylessly settling into the sacrificial role of her mother's caretaker.

Last year Evelyn's mother died. Rather than being released from her sense of waste and loss, as some friends and family hoped would happen, Evelyn is increasingly immobilized, anxious, and bitter. It isn't easy to relinquish entrenched habits and behavior, even those that have clearly limited our lives. The void created by new circumstances presses to be filled; and as we know, confronting the unfamiliar can be genuinely alarming for many people.

Will Evelyn, for example, have to make a greater effort

now to live in the present? Perhaps examine her fears about seeking love and intimacy in a way she never had to when she consigned such experiences to an irretrievable past? Evelyn senses, and it deepens her anxiety and pain, that her obsessive concentration on the past made a prison of regret, robbing her of the initiative she needed to control the flow of immediate experience.

Continually imagining what might have been allows us to avoid the need to do something constructive in the present, or build hopes for the future. Clearly, though, staying stuck in the mistakes of the past as a way to avoid today's imperfect life is not a healthy defense against emotional pain. Regret will only deepen and intensify, as the present never improves and every day adds dimension to the unlived life.

Besides this faulty group of defenses, there are other kinds of defensive behavior people use along the bumpy road of self-deception. For instance, Karen Horney describes the role "false pride" plays in avoiding the admission that we have fallen short of our idealized selves. We cling to false pride whenever we try to avert our eyes from the absence of certain idealized character traits. The man who fears emotional dependence may take inordinate pride in being totally self-sufficient; a woman who feels she can't handle career success celebrates her complete dedication to marriage and motherhood. Any confrontation with the falseness of our boast is anxiously avoided, because that would make us see an aspect of ourselves that we have learned to fear and be ashamed of.

To varying degrees we all try to avoid looking at aspects of ourselves that might disturb an idealized image. The more unrealistic our ideal view of ourselves is, however, the more we will deny any response or experience that doesn't support it. Connected to this idea of false pride concerning unrealistic goals is an inappropriate *sense of entitlement* in life, or what Karen Horney sees as *exaggerated claims*.

Unlike healthy needs, such as the legitimate need for love

and meaningful work, these claims are based on needs that are excessive, irrational, and unrealistic. With an exaggerated sense of entitlement, we can feel it's our due to have all wishes fulfilled, with little appreciation of what efforts these goals may require from us. The claims become defensive strategies to avoid honest self-perception or appraisal of what we really need to do to reach our goals and make life vital and rewarding. Regret accumulates over our choices as we neglect to take the steps that will make them work out.

For example, we may choose the right college or job for our particular intellectual and career needs, but if we assume we can coast by and don't have to work very hard to compete, opportunity can slip into failure, and self-confidence into bewildered disappointment.

Love is an especially fertile ground for the playing out of unrealistic claims, both consciously and unconsciously. We may expect a partner to be always loving and fulfill all our needs, without doing much ourselves to keep the relationship vital. When our mates or lovers don't feel or respond the way we'd like them to, we get frustrated and angry, and may even want to get back at them for not reinforcing a sense of our own perfection and importance.

We all harbor at least some unrealistic claims on life— once again particularly today, when the culture promotes too many choices and encourages greed and a sense of self-centered entitlement. Thus, more than ever, it is important to try to recognize when we are making irrational demands on life, so that we don't feel aggrieved and bitterly regretful when we don't get what we want. If we are consumed by regret over some disappointing outcome, it's helpful to examine our frustration to see whether its degree is appropriate to the reality of the situation. Feelings of extreme resentment are often clues to the fact that we are hanging on to unrealistic claims that are creating a need to retaliate in some way for what is in truth a quite legitimate setback.

Sometimes we feel tension from a belief system that is incompatible with our behavior, rather than from a failure to get what we think we're entitled to. Psychologist Leon Festinger explains the theory of "cognitive dissonance," in which there is a discrepancy between our behavior and our real beliefs, or between opposing belief systems. A tension is created that we try to reduce by bringing these two elements—our belief system and our actual behavior—closer together. For example, the nervousness we feel about smoking when we know that it's bad for our health can be reduced either by changing behavior—stopping smoking—or by changing our beliefs, finding justifications to continue the behavior. ("I always gain weight when I stop smoking, and that's bad for me also.")

A graphic illustration of this process, as it relates to denying regret, was witnessed when Betty Friedan first identified the "feminine mystique." She exposed the confusion of countless women trying to cope with unhappiness over lives that were supposed to be filled with contentment. They had achieved what they had been told was a woman's ultimate success—marriage, family, house in a comfortable suburb—and still they felt a malaise.

In large part, their distress stemmed from the dissonance between their ongoing domestic behavior and their emerging dissatisfaction with the traditional female role. To reduce this tension, many women tried to suppress their real attitudes and make them more consistent with conventional definitions of a "woman's place." However, when Ms. Friedan came along, offering an explanation of "the problem that had no name," many of these same women were able to understand why they were unhappy and now, instead of trying to deny their feelings, addressed their unhappiness by beginning to change their conditioned female behavior.

Research into regret supports the view that there is always a tendency to justify the choices we have made. After making an important or irreversible life decision, like quitting a job or having a child, we naturally try to bolster the choice by reassuring ourselves that it was the only possible right one. This stratagem can be helpful to peace of mind, but if it is carried too far, the roots of self-deception can take hold, keeping us from taking an honest look at how we feel about our lives.

As Edith Wharton said, we are all, inevitably, "blunderers." But as we go on living and growing, "we have to set to work, and build up, little by little, bit by bit, the precious things we'd smashed to atoms without knowing it." Whether through outright denial of our blunders or other self-deceiving strategies, our current attempts to disavow regret speak to our discomfort about modern life's extraordinary number of options. There appears to be a collective longing to avoid the disquieting idea that our choices are uncertain and rife with consequence.

While such hesitation is understandable, insight is the principal key to choosing well and to coping with regret if our choices fail. Self-deception may protect us for a while from painful truths about what we've done or failed to be, but it also keeps us from making some level of peace with the person we are and can still become.

JOURNEYING THROUGH LIFE

How can I teach, how can I save,
This child whose features are my own,
Whose feet run down the ways where
I have walked?

—MICHAEL ROBERTS

FIVE

When Regret Begins

"Last summer I was in the Grand Canyon with my family, and they all went swimming in a beautiful stream under a giant waterfall. I wanted to go in with them. I can swim okay but not great. (I quit swimming class when my brother and me took lessons, because I got tired of hearing everybody say what a great swimmer he was becoming.)

"There were a whole bunch of kids going through the falls that day, and I didn't want to freak out in front of them if I got scared about not making it. So I told my father that I wanted to go for a hike instead, but what I really did was stand behind a tree and watch everybody in the water, and I felt lousy because they were all having so much fun. Now, it feels like nobody in my family ever even mentions swimming without someone else remembering how great that day in the canyon was. I wish I had gone in with them." Fourteen-year-old Jeff's words come tumbling out in a troubled rush.

The experience of regret begins in childhood, even though it is a time when life's possibilities seem infinite. Many of us don't like to think of children feeling regretful; it flies in the face of the popular myth of the happy, carefree child. The sometimes harsh reality of our own adult lives deepens our need to believe in myth.

Often disappointed, we want our children to be hopeful. Disillusioned by love, we hope that our children will never have to question love's benevolence. Troubled by guilt, we recoil at the idea that anything we might have said would "lay a guilt trip" on our own children. Saddened by regret, we want our children to retain youth's beguiling sense of omnipotence and eager air of promise.

As part of our research we surveyed more than eight hundred children from kindergarten through high school to discover when the sense of regret first begins to form and what kinds of regret are most common to the process of growing up. No similar investigation had ever been made, probably because the linkage of children and regret is so incompatible to traditional thinking. Yet we were startled to discover that no matter how much we might like to believe otherwise, the seeds of regret are sown very early in children's lives. What's more, as we get older and struggle with adult regret, our feelings are very likely rooted in those early emotional experiences.

There is a remarkable similarity between the situations that cause regret in childhood and those that challenge us in maturity.

If our lives touch the life of a child, as a parent, a teacher, or merely as a member of society eager to make the world a better place for future generations, it's important that we help children develop the capacity to make constructive choices. Today more than ever, to be an able caretaker to children as they mature requires helping them gain a progressive understanding that life is a series of choices, and that choice always carries some level of consequence.

As children grow older, we can guide them toward also accepting increasing responsibility for their decisions and the consequences that follow. Journalist Sidney J. Harris sees this sense of responsibility as a major factor in the definition of maturity: "We have not passed that subtle line between childhood and adulthood," he says, "until we move from the passive voice to the active voice—that is, until we have stopped saying, 'It got lost,' and say, 'I lost it.' "

To start children down the road to such maturity, we need to hear the important messages behind their stories of deceptively simple experience. If we listen we can recognize regret when it first appears, and glimpse its early relationship to choice. We can use this knowledge not only to guide boys and girls through the complex terrain of a contemporary childhood, but to help them sort out their evolving set of values and the decisions they may be led to.

If children gradually learn that what they do now will affect how they feel about themselves later on, they will be more prepared for the expanded options of adolescence and young adulthood. They will be more aware of the importance of basing their choices on genuine needs and emerging healthy values.

We found three main areas of experience that arouse regret in children. In Jeff's wistful, uncomfortable sense of being an outsider because of his discomfort over deep water, we see the first source of regret: *an early fear of risk-taking that evolves into a lifelong, life-limiting shape.*

"Myself and fear were born twins," wrote the seventeenth-century philosopher Thomas Hobbes, recognizing how *fear, perhaps more than any other emotion, touches life from the moment of birth.*

There are many kinds of fears connected to a fear of risk-taking in both adults and children:

A fear of the unknown
A fear of looking foolish or failing
A fear of fantasized worst-case scenarios
A fear of hurting others
A fear of not being liked, or being rejected
A fear of being abandoned

All these anxieties, which keep us from trying new experiences, were responses that came up over and over again, even from young children. We were frankly surprised that so many children wished they had persisted in doing something that appealed to them but also frightened them because the outcome was unknown. "I wish I had more courage to do stuff," summed up Bobby, a second-grader. "I wish I went in the Haunted House in Disney World when we went on our vacation. I didn't because I was afraid." If an eight-year-old lacks the courage to enter an amusement park's haunted house or, later, as an adolescent, can't ask a classmate to a school dance, he is clearly having experiences that parallel the frightening challenges of adulthood.

How we resolve these first difficult battles with our fearful selves creates lifelong attitudes toward both finding courage and having compassion for our fears.

If a parent appears to disapprove of a child's fear, waving it away or becoming irritated at its expression, it's very likely the child will become silently anxious about a feeling that still torments her. A far more constructive approach is to encourage children to share their feelings, even the most irrational fear. As child psychotherapist Clark Moustakis explains, "The value of talking lies less in the particular content and more in the freedom to talk. The child who gains the freedom to talk has gained the freedom to share himself."

Unless we encourage and genuinely accept even disclosures that are painful to hear, children can bring along into adulthood a sense that to be afraid is wrong and shameful. In a culture that seems preoccupied with boldness and courage, this sense of shame can lead to futile attempts to deny or hide fear that imprisons us in face-saving but emotionally unrewarding maneuvers. Had fourteen-year-old Jeff not been so ashamed of his fears, for example, he might have been able to ask his mother or father to help him risk swimming through the waterfall by swimming along beside him.

To the degree that children continue to hide their fear of failure, humiliation, and rejection, they are less likely to make choices that help them develop a sense of mastery over their lives. We need to help children understand that even irrational feelings and a sense of vulnerability are part of any sensitive person's occasional response to life. *The most successful way for children to grow into adults who can tolerate risk is for them to feel that not only is it all right to be afraid of risk-taking, but that courage lies in admitting our fears and trying to face them as best we can.*

Dr. Arthur Jersild, a prominent psychoanalyst and children's advocate, gives another reason why airing childhood fears is important. His explanation calls to mind the unfortunate adult tendency to believe that other people are happier than we are: "When a frightened child feels free to express his fright, and is struck by the fact that others also are afraid, at least a small dent has been made in the vicious chain of fear and blame through which [he] becomes alienated from others and from himself."

It is immensely helpful and often very surprising for children to discover that other children feel shy or lonely and afraid—even that they also share the particularly heart-stopping dread of making a fool of themselves in some public exposure.

Another famous psychoanalyst, Alfred Adler, once observed that many children grow up "in the constant dread of being laughed at." This is also a fear that can travel along with us into adult life, eroding the playfulness that can lighten the sometimes dense climate of grown-up reality. As one woman of sixty-eight told us after her husband had suffered a massive stroke: "[Before the stroke] he was always trying to get me to be more playful. He had a wonderful, childlike love of games and make-believe, but I never let myself go enough to respond to him. What I wouldn't give for him to be vital and healthy enough now for us to just have fun together!"

A fear of looking silly or different can crush children's natural inclinations and restrict their choices. "I wish I'd joined up with the ice-skating team even though most of the skaters were girls. I was afraid the other boys would think I was queer," says thirteen-year-old Billy, while an eleven-year-old girl tells us: "My mother wanted to buy me a really unusual dress for the class party, and I loved it, but then I thought it might look too weird, so I bought a dress that was just like everyone else's, and now I feel terrible that I didn't get something I liked just because it was different."

Another fear connected to taking risks that troubles children is a fear of rejection and of not being liked. When, as adults, we regret that in spite of our hunger for deep relationships, we seem unable to reach out because of too little confidence and self-esteem, we can often trace the dilemma to the perplexing interpersonal experiences of childhood. Jules Henry, the anthropologist, explains about children and friends: "The fact that everyone can be chosen or rejected . . . makes for enormous uncertainty in interpersonal relations; it makes for great sensitivity to looks, stares, smiles, and criticism, and originates the endless inner questioning, 'Am I liked?' "

Susie, an eighth-grader, fed her fear of rejection with worst-case scenarios, which ultimately reinforced her sense of isolation. She recalled her recent discomfort in the locker room when her classmates chattered and shrieked with laughter about some shared excitement during a recent school trip to Washington. Susie didn't go to Washington, because "I didn't think anyone would want to hang out with me there, and I thought everyone would see I didn't have any friends."

Children have a great need for companionship, but anxiety that comes from fantasies of rejection can make friendship seem fraught with risk. A self-fulfilling prophecy may take shape as the socially awkward child grows tempted to avoid new social experiences rather than chance being rebuffed. In a society so outwardly gregarious, the relatively friendless child feels a particular loss of self-esteem. This is why many children (and adults) will take an opposite tack, throwing themselves into a great number of superficial friendships rather than forming fewer but more intimate relationships.

Parents can help children understand the real value of friendship, which has nothing to do with numbers, and ease a child's fears about finding close companions if they don't place too high a value themselves on being popular. It can be very disconcerting for parents to hear about their child's fear of rejection, for it often touches off personally painful social memories. However, we need to separate our experience from what our children are feeling so that they are free to talk about their fears without our own unproductive overreacting.

If we believe it ourselves, we can also show children the brighter side of what some might call loneliness. Many of the most sensitive, creative, and intellectually aware children we talked to spent a great deal of time alone. Being left to their own interests made them particularly free to discover what those interests might be. As psychoanalyst Anthony Storr observed about children who were comfortable being alone, "The capacity to be alone . . . becomes linked with self-discovery and self-realization; with becoming aware of one's deepest needs, feelings and impulses."

Indeed, many people who have made major contributions to the world had quite isolated childhoods. Albert Einstein wrote, for example, "For the most part, I do the thing which my own nature drives me to do. . . . I live in that solitude which is painful in youth, but delicious in the years of maturity."

If the first source of childhood regret is the fears connected to risk-taking, *the second major source of regret for children is the failure to seize an important moment.* With a lifetime ahead of them, children still seem to sense the sadness and loss of letting an important moment in life go by. There are many experiences they wish to relive, to act before the chance to act the way they really wanted to was gone:

"I wish I had put together the present my grandfather gave me before he got so sick, because he always asked if I finished putting it together and now he's too sick to know even if I did." (Paulette, age eight)

"I wish I had rescued my cat and made him my pet right

after his owners dumped him and not let him stay in the alley next door for so long while he got hungry and all scared." (Brian, age nine)

Even very young children exhibit the raw beginnings of regret over letting an important moment with another person pass by. A three-year-old named Sam waited with his mother outside their home for the school bus to pick up Josh, his six-year-old brother. As the bus turned the corner, Josh kissed his mother goodbye and then, in a burst of good feeling, leaned down to kiss Sam, who scowled and pushed him away.

When the bus pulled off with his big brother inside, Sam burst into tears. His face was crimson with anguish, his voice choked as he sobbed to his mother that he'd changed his mind—he wanted to kiss Josh goodbye. At age three, it's highly unlikely that a developed sense of guilt motivated Sam's tears. What is much more plausible is that he was feeling some genuine sadness, not so much for rejecting his brother as for his own loss. Experience had already shown Sam how good Josh's embrace made him feel, but nothing Sam could do would make the departing bus turn around so that he could have that good feeling again.

The results of our survey of children's regrets about not seizing the moment is consistent with our observation of adults and regret: *The road not taken is more often the source of pain for children than the road unhappily traveled.*

In adolescence, these regrets become more complex and, in part because they do contain some guilt, are even more intensely felt. "When my grandma lived with my family, I didn't treat her very nicely at all. I treated her as though she didn't exist sometimes. I loved her, but I just didn't realize how great she was. Now she's in a nursing home far away, near my aunt's house, and I never see her. I wish I had shown her I loved her." (Joni, age thirteen)

Fourteen-year-old Hallie describes bidding her father and new stepmother a carefully casual goodbye after they took her to the airport, ending a vacation visit. She remembered feeling sad as she looked back at them while she walked toward the gate. As soon as the plane took off, she wrote in her diary, "I wish I had told my stepmother I really liked the things she tried to do for me."

Hallie's story was not at all uncommon in our research into the lives of modern children trying to adjust to splintered family relationships and new marital arrangements. It may soothe some of the confusion and hurt of step- and divorced parents to realize that the son or daughter trying to feel comfortable with the new family script (and change of cast) may actually understand that real effort is being made in their behalf, but, like Hallie, they can't always articulate appreciation because everyone's new coming together is still too emotionally charged.

Another form of regret related to the road not taken is in *not having tried harder and done better in school*. This is identical to our own and other research findings that adults deeply regret not having worked harder or made more of their educational opportunities. In remarkably similar scenarios, boys and girls look back with regret at their lack of commitment to earlier learning, a finding that should help parents weather their children's relentless complaints about practicing or homework.

A bright nine-year-old boy, already longing for the rewards of external recognition, says, "I wish I studied harder to get more awards." And a seventeen-year-old girl who always took pride in being able to slide through her classes without pushing herself now faces the regrettable results of that earlier attitude toward learning. "I want to go to an expensive private college instead of the state university. I wish I had tried harder academically in high school. I always did well, but I never put more than seventy-five percent of real work into what I did. If I had worked harder then, I might have been able to get a scholarship now to help with college tuition."

It doesn't have to be formal schooling that stirs these regrets. Many adults, for example, wish they had been serious about music lessons or practiced more at sports, and children will also berate themselves for neglecting their talents. Lisa, age sixteen, looks back on her life and regrets "how easy it was to quit things I didn't enjoy, like dance or gymnastics or guitar. I should have stuck with at least one of them and really gotten *good* at something," she says plaintively, and then adds: "My mother was talking to my dad the other night about how one of her friends was so *dedicated* to her job helping retarded children. I thought that was such a great word. . . . That's what I wish I was . . . a *dedicated* person who did something they really cared about the very best way there was!"

In fact, a parent or other concerned adult could help Lisa realize that it is not too late to dedicate herself to some pursuit she really cares about. This is exactly the power regret has to prompt change.

On the other hand, when Duane was fifteen years old he was placed in advanced Latin and science classes in high school. He also began to take an art class that really excited him and soon decided that he wanted to transfer to less competitive academic classes so that he'd have more time to devote to painting. His parents resisted his wishes at first, but finally agreed to the shift, although with unmistakable disapproval.

While Duane and Lisa seem to be on the opposite ends of a spectrum—with Lisa regretting not making a long-term investment in a creative ability and Duane deciding that in terms of real fulfillment, the principle of sticking it out can backfire—they are not really far apart. Faced with the multiple choices of modern life, both young people must learn to think through, and then thoughtfully decide, whether a goal is legitimate and worth pursuing.

To help a child answer such a question, parents must first examine their own feelings of disappointment at the child's response, to see if they have invested too much of their own ambitions in a son's or a daughter's carrying out a particular activity. While many adults feel stick-to-itiveness is the way to teach a child responsibility, it can often be counterproductive to push children into following through on something they genuinely dislike or even sometimes feel demoralized by: "I wish I had never stayed so long at dancing school and not taken so much putting down from the other kids because all it did was make me feel clumsy and bitter." (Stephanie, age seventeen)

Once we have grappled with our own motivations, we may be better able to let our children consider whether indeed their perseverance has become an obligatory pursuit, primarily toward someone else's goals. They should then feel free to arrive at a conclusion that might sound blasphemous in a culture that demands unbounded achievement: There are times when the most appropriate and advisable action is to quit.

The feeling that other people (usually our parents) know what is best for us, and we are afraid to displease them, can lead a young person into the illusion of no choice and its painful potential for self-blame.

Perry, a bright nineteen-year-old, deeply regrets that he succumbed to his father's wish that he live at home and attend a local college. "I was offered a scholarship there, and my parents were saying I should take it, that I was stupid to turn it down. They would much rather put the money aside for me that they would have spent on board if I had gone away to school, so that I could have a nest egg when I graduated. Sure, it made a lot of sense. The problem was, I didn't want to be a commuting student. I had dreamed about campus life for years.

"I agreed too quickly to their choice, because I didn't think then that they could really be wrong, or that I had a right to feel the way I did if they couldn't see my point of view. I should have tried to deal with their disapproval. . . . I should have risked their disappointment. I would tell parents that to be in their kid's camp is the best thing of all, even if the kid's decisions turn out to be wrong. I know parents probably feel, like mine did, that their choices are more sensible, but in the long run it's us who have to live with these decisions and we may not really want to."

Psychiatrist and author Thomas Szasz has noted that "a

child becomes an adult when he realizes that he has a right not only to be right but also to be wrong." Yet many parents are extremely reluctant to allow their children to make their own mistakes. As noted Swiss psychoanalyst Alice Miller has observed in her extensive work on childhood, children are often expected to comply unilaterally with their parents' wishes and expectations. This can mean that not only the child's own preferences but certain feelings are deemed unacceptable.

The end result of such control by a parent, says Dr. Miller, can be that children grow into adulthood afraid to express their true feelings or, worse, won't know what their true feelings are. As one woman in her forties told us: "I have no idea what it takes to make me happy. . . . I have regrets about my life, but I wouldn't know how to change things to make them go away."

It is crucial to fight against the natural desire to view our children as extensions of ourselves, rather than as separate and unique beings with the right to independent actions, feelings, temperaments, and interests—or even the lack of them.

Writing in *The New York Times*, Professor Andrew Merton described his excitement at taking his four-year-old son, Gabe, to a major league ball game. His pleasure was abruptly curtailed when, well before the game began, after watching batting practice and eating some snacks, his son announced, "I think I've had enough baseball. I want to go home now."

Professor Merton recalled his anger at the boy's stubborn insistence on leaving, and how upset he was that Gabe didn't share his idea of a wonderful afternoon. However, as Merton began the drive home in stony silence, he passed a museum that Gabe had recently enjoyed visiting. Grudgingly, the father suggested that they might stop there again, and the little boy enthusiastically agreed.

As they wandered through the museum Mr. Merton's feelings greatly changed. "I acknowledged to myself how much I wanted Gabe to be like me. He was supposed to like the baseball game, not for his sake, but for mine, and I had gotten angry at him when he didn't measure up to my expectations."

He went on to say that he also realized that he had been engaged in a battle of wills with his son, a battle he now was grateful that Gabe had won. The child had "stood up for what he thought was right," explains Merton, and: "Son and father, together, had saved the day—he by holding out for something he enjoyed and I by having the sense, finally, to realize that he was right, and to let go of my dream of how things should be."

This story graphically illustrates the need for parents to listen—genuinely listen—to their children's feelings and preferences, and to support them as much as possible. The early years are the time for learning how to deal with the important dilemma of self versus other, approval versus autonomy, and we encourage this process by trying hard not to interfere too much with the natural unfolding of a child's unique personality.

The third prominent area of regret in childhood deals with issues of control. These may range from situations where children could in fact exercise some control, to those where no control is truly possible.

We noted an intriguing use of symbolic example when children talked about a lack of control. Many of the boys and girls were unhappy about not being able to change their bedrooms to suit their tastes. While this may at first seem a rather trivial regret, if we think of the child's room as a microcosm of the larger world, we can understand how distressing it is to have no choice in how one's bedroom is arranged or decorated.

"I want to hang a lot of stuff on the walls," a seven-year-old boy named Keith told us, "but Mommy says it looks too sloppy. I like sloppy, but I know it's bad," he adds with a conforming sigh. Keith has had no choice but to accept his mother's definitions of bad and good.

Children who are rarely allowed to make value judgments or to act on those judgments often grow into people who seek approval through their choices and who rigidly divide experience into black and white, right and wrong. Their lives are thus mine fields of potential regret, for they cannot risk any choice that is in the least uncertain or ambiguous.

We do not mean to imply that children don't ever need to succumb to adult decisions, or that limits should not be set for them, but only that adults should try to encourage children's own sense of mastery. After all, there are so many situations in which, unlike decorating a room, it is impossible for them to gain control over experience.

Many youthful regrets stem from not having the ability to change parental behavior that causes a child emotional or physical pain. At their most extreme, these would involve actual child abuse. But they also range from parents working too much and being unavailable ("I can't stop my daddy from going on business trips; I wish he could be home more" [Bruce, age nine]), to fear about parents smoking or drinking ("I can't control that my mom drinks too much; when she drinks she fights with my father and with us kids" [Lilli, age fourteen]), to family feuds that shatter previously loving relationships.

"My father had a fight with my uncle," says Chris, age nine, fighting off tears. "My dad gets mad if I say I miss my uncle, but I do. We used to go to the movies together, and once he took me away just with him on a camping trip. My dad's mad at him, not me. Why do I have to act like I'm mad too?"

Chris's father would be well advised to consider this question. As members of the family, children need to have their feelings considered, including their anger at adult behavior. And if changes in these behaviors can be made, it would be a useful way to bring some sense of control to the child's world.

The issue of anger is important in the story of childhood regret. A surprising number of children listed their inability to control their tempers as something they wished they could change. While some of these children did actually have major tantrums, in other instances what they reported as examples of their "temper" seemed merely clumsy attempts at self-assertion. They felt they were out of bounds about what seemed to us reasonable demands, which may reflect the intolerance of adults toward any expression of anger from a child.

The constructive expression of anger is one of the most important tools that children use in shaping a sense of values. The demands they make, the rights they defend, their resistance to people who frustrate or hurt them, are initially stirred by anger. Learning in childhood what kind of angry expression is appropriate and what is not will help keep them from confusing self-assertion with aggression when they become adults.

If we remember that adults greatly regret *not being assertive enough*, we can understand how important it is for children to grow up feeling that it is acceptable to feel—and at certain moments to act—angry, but that lashing out in anger is not the true definition of self-assertion.

Anger often does lead both adults and children to lash out meanly at another person, an action that to a surprising degree young people revealed as a regret: "I punched my brother in the face and I felt sick when his nose bled." (Louis, age eight) "I teased my friend and made her feel bad. She had only one best friend, me, and I made her cry. I wish I hadn't done it." (Miriam, age seven) "Last year, when I was in the fifth grade, I was in the 'in group,' and I was mean to people that weren't in the group too. I'm sorry I was mean because now they are my real friends—not like some people I used to know." (Ellen, age eleven) "I wish I could be nicer to my brother and certain animals." (George, age five)

Fourteen-year-old Alex refused to ask his longtime best friend to his birthday party because they'd had a quarrel. "I'm not going to go sucking up to him. . . . I'm not going to be the one to apologize." The party took place and was obviously joyless for its host. Later, Alex told his mother: "I should have invited Robbie to the party. He's going to feel lousy when everyone talks about it at school." When Alex's mother tried to comfort him by saying he could invite Robbie to something else, he waved her assurances away. "I won't have another birthday party for a year," Alex grimly reminded her.

Although Alex's mother was trying to ease his guilt, her efforts were unsuccessful because she seemed to make light of a situation that to him was extremely serious. In situations like this, when children regret an action that caused someone else pain, it is preferable for parents to acknowledge their feelings and, in appropriate language and without producing guilt, move the child toward the understanding that our behavior carries both responsibility and consequence.

"I didn't learn to swim, because of my appearance; I stayed away from . . . the pond beyond the poorhouse, and from the public pool . . . and the indoor pool at the Reading 'Y,' " John Updike writes in "At War with My Skin." He had contracted psoriasis in kindergarten, and the "red spots, ripening into slivery scabs" shaped the writer's childhood and the rest of his life by imposing on him tremendous self-consciousness about his physical appearance.

Updike is describing the kind of regret and resentment that children often feel results from a cruel trick of fate. While they can try to modify their physical appearance and personal characteristics, childhood is shadowed by these aspects of self that are beyond their control.

"I wish I was tall and had lots of muscles," says Joel, stocky and short for the age of eleven. "Girls like tall skinny boys." Sixteen-year-old Dana is harshly specific about her alleged lacks. "I would change my looks: I would have a thinner nose, blue eyes, and more curves in the right places." "I have this awful laugh," says another eleven-year-old. "I gulp and make noises like a horse." He closes his eyes in disgust. For children with physical or learning handicaps, these regrets can be quite acute. "I hate having asthma," says eight-year-old Leon, "I can't do half the things that the other kids do in gym."

The pain of regret over a faulty self-image can be enormously restricting to childhood and adolescent contentment. A University of California study showed 58 percent of seventeen-year-old girls believed they were overweight, when only 17 percent actually were. Nine-year-old girls already worriedly followed diets to conform to this society that worships thinness, and braces were a cross to bear for countless children in our survey. "My teeth grew and I couldn't control them and now I have these ugly braces," said a twelve-year-old boy morosely. Unresolved in childhood, these negative feelings about our appearance trail us into adult life, almost insuring even deeper regret especially at stages of aging when we detect signs of physical decline.

The regrets that are most painful in childhood are often the ones that are absolutely beyond the child's control, in particular those that result from death and divorce. When a beloved grandparent is suddenly and permanently gone, it is overwhelming to both young and older children, and of course the loss of a mother, father, or sibling is usually even more intensely felt. In families where religious ties are strong, it is often easier to cope with loss. Fourteen-year-old Katie says, for example, "I miss my grandpa very much, but I still try to keep God number one. I know that there is a reason for everything."

Yet, even when there is such religious conviction about a hidden meaning in loss, and certainly when such conviction is absent, death can bring the regrets of unfinished business to children of every age:

"I wish I told my mom I loved her before she died," says Stevie, age twelve. His voice is thick with grief. His mother's illness was protracted and frightening and Stevie found it hard to visit her and watch her decline.

The yearning to have expressed love before a person died is strikingly common and, among other children, was often tied to regret for not having participated in the ritual of saying goodbye: "My grandmother died (my close grandmother), and I didn't get to go to the funeral. I wish I'd went there and seen her before she was buried." (Rosie, age eleven) And a seventeen-year-old looks back on her life and confirms this need for a ritualized way of accepting loss: "If I could do it over, I would go to all of the wakes that I missed when I was younger so I could see the people dead, and know in my mind that they are gone, and not have their deaths lingering in my mind."

We may be understandably tempted to protect our children from what we see as the harsh reality of funerals and wakes, but as these comments make clear, some children seem to need to participate in these events to help them through the process of grieving.

The losses of death, premature or otherwise, have always been part of life. But we have never before known the degree of divorce and separation that we experience today. These losses are particularly bitter to the child dependent on family life for security and survival. We have to expect that our children will be wrestling with unresolved feelings of resentment and abandonment, even sometimes a sense that they are responsible for the split. Though we may genuinely believe that, overall, divorce is the best solution to family problems, from a child's view divorce is more often than not a catastrophe.

"My parents' divorce seems like the biggest waste of time and sadness in my life," says a fourteen-year-old girl. And a young man named Lenny, about to conclude a very productive experience in therapy, recalls with bitter vividness his parents' divorce when he was seven. Because his mother wanted to go to law school in another state, his father took on full-time custody.

"I loved my father, and he probably was the most stable parent for me at the time, but I couldn't get over the feeling that my mother really didn't love me or she wouldn't have left.

"I remember as if it was yesterday, waking up in the middle of the night soon after she'd moved, feeling sick. My room was dark and chilly, and my stomach and head hurt, and I started to cry and call out for my mother. Suddenly there was a flash of light, and my father was standing in the doorway in his robe. Up until that moment I had forgotten she was gone. But in that moment I realized I couldn't call out for her anymore. The bleakness of that idea, the terror of it, can't be described."

Lenny is using his childhood regrets productively. He is determined to build a family for himself that will be committed to providing security for the children he hopes to have.

"I regret deeply that I had so much pain as a child, but I'm not looking for another woman to make up to me for what I feel my mother cheated me of. Therapy has helped me to understand her needs and, even more important, that feeling sorry for myself forever isn't much of a life. It's much more productive to use my childhood pain to become a better parent myself."

Although childhood regret is experienced by both boys and girls, there are some gender distinctions to be made. In their extensive research into the development of women, Jean Baker Miller and Carol Gilligan discovered that a girl's definition of herself grows out of her attachment to others. Consequently, the choices she makes are often to protect relationships. This tendency toward discounting her own true feelings and wishes in deference to someone else's, or to what she thinks someone else wants from her, begins early in life.

For example, a twelve-year-old girl told us: "I wish I'd gone camping with my brother, but I didn't want to leave my mom at home. She's still sad over my daddy leaving us." Her fourteen-year-old brother is a charming, caring boy, but, unlike his sister, he had no real conflict about following his natural inclinations and leaving his mother to go camping. Boys are typically encouraged to separate from their mothers, to be more autonomous, and to make independent decisions.

These traditionally "male" characteristics may help sow the frequent masculine regrets of not being able to express emotional need or develop truly intimate friendships, but not the regrets that are shaped by female self-effacement. The girl who stayed home with her mother, even though she was the younger sibling, had already begun to suppress her own desires on behalf of what she perceived as someone else's need. A pattern of this kind of behavior can ultimately stunt emotional growth and lead to a life paralyzed by obligation, sometimes encouraging the passive-aggressive behavior of the person who feels too powerless to assert her own needs. It is not surprising, then, that when women of any age regret not taking risks, their pain is often linked to self-sacrifice.

Male or female, "the most important problem for any young person's life is to have models to suggest possibilities," wrote Joseph Campbell, while cautioning that "the mind has many possibilities, but we can live no more than one life."

There are no replays in life, but we can help children make the most of their one life's options. No matter what roads they take or turn away from, we can offer them a sense that their lives are not predetermined but contain the many possibilities inherent in the notion of free will.

Children who understand the implications of choosing one path over another can build a value system that establishes their own priorities regarding what is important and less important, what they need now and what they can wait for, and what set of choices are worthy of risk.

If, as adults, we stand in the shadows of our childhood regrets, then fostering such self-awareness and responsibility of choice cannot come too soon in a child's life. Recognizing regret early, using it instead of fearing it, can create adults who are able to avoid both the greedy, futile need to "have it all" and the bleak "safety" of such limited options that their one life is never fully lived.

"You are the only young man that I know of who ignores the fact that the future becomes the present, the present the past, and the past turns into everlasting regret if you don't plan for it!"

—Amanda to her son, in *The Glass Menagerie*
by TENNESSEE WILLIAMS

SIX

The Regrets of Young Adulthood

Rebecca arrives for our interview wearing a typical "dress-for-success" suit, but when she removes her jacket, instead of a tailored blouse we are surprised to see a colorful T-shirt. Its cartoon illustration shows a woman clasping a hand to her forehead in dismay. Above her head, a balloon contains her horrified thoughts: "I . . . I can't believe it. I forgot to have children!"

Rebecca is director of subsidiary rights at a large publishing house. Her work regularly spills over into her social life, with book parties, conventions, and lots of "hanging out" in bars and restaurants that attract other publishing people. She is rarely without male or female companionship, and when she's feeling in the mood for more impassioned connections, she seldom has trouble linking up with a man for more serious, albeit temporary, commitments. Suddenly, however, her life seems to be losing some of its luster.

"I'm thirty-eight years old," she says, sounding troubled,

"and I've never really had a deeply committed relationship with a man. I've never even tried to have one. It was something I thought would just naturally happen at the right time. But when is the right time? I have this awful feeling that time is running out!"

Traveling through her twenties, Rebecca came to many crossroads marked by signposts that were—as they commonly are—unclear. Usually she would turn away from one road and plunge down another without breaking her swift stride long enough to consider the implications of her choice.

"I look back now to my twenties," she says, "and I can see that I made certain decisions—and decisions of omission—that altered the shape of my life. Without really thinking it through, I got onto a fast professional track that made me abandon my early fantasies of having an academic career. The harder I worked at my job, the less time I gave to keeping up old interests and friendships whose diversity might have broadened my life . . . and the more successful I got, the more expensive my life-style became, so that even if I did have second thoughts about being so enmeshed in my career, I have to work as hard as I do just to sustain myself."

Rebecca's sense of being boxed in by previous choices illustrates why regret, or at least its beginnings, is such a potential of young adulthood. In our twenties and thirties, *despite our tenuous grip on maturity, we are constantly making decisions about our careers and personal life that will direct the course of the rest of adult life.* The jobs we take, the lovers we reject, the marriages we make, the relationships we retreat from, the education we continue or abandon, the creativity we encourage or put aside, how we change the connections to our parents, becoming parents ourselves, all form the crucially important options and create the life structure of early adulthood.

No wonder Rebecca wore that T-shirt. She is just as perplexed as its cartoon lady by the idea that certain decisions can't be indefinitely postponed, and also by her realization that even choices that seemed right at the time may have unwelcome repercussions. "It isn't that I'm unhappy with my life." Rebecca summed up her feelings with a sigh. "It's just that I wish I'd had a better sense of where my life was going while it was still being formed."

Rebecca's wistful reflections about where her choices have led brings to mind a passage from Ernest Hemingway's novel *The Garden of Eden.* "If I didn't love you for anything else, I'd love you for your decisions," the newlywed Catherine tells her young husband, David. With precocious wisdom, David replies, "They're easy to make when you haven't seen how too many of them can turn out."

Young adults will inevitably, as Hemingway suggests, make decisions in a partial vacuum. Their experience in the world is still limited, providing less than a full range of vision with which to judge the course of their journey. As young adults, we are still consolidating our various roles into a whole that feels integrated rather than fragmented, still grappling with our personal and social values, still establishing our priorities. Added to this is the pressure of cultural expectations of when and how we should take on adult responsibilities in family and career.

Other periods of life have their own requirements and options, but considering the significance of the demands and opportunities of the early adult years, it's not surprising that our twenties and thirties are such an intense phase of the life cycle. At our biologic peak, we feel our greatest energy and are full of passion and ambition. Our impulses may seem filled with contradiction, creating both enormous excitement and sometimes overwhelming stress as we swing back and forth between conflicting desires and emotional states.

Our current system of values adds a particular complication to the challenges of early adulthood by celebrating men and women who seem to have burst into full adult power overnight. They star in huge-budget films, control multimillion-dollar stock deals. Barely out of college, they write best sellers, advise presidential candidates, create persuasive advertising campaigns that earn them more than a presidential salary. If we measure ourselves against these whiz kids, we can feel terribly wanting.

In truth, the whiz kids themselves may share our discomfort.

Cy is twenty-nine and a vice-president on Wall Street. He enjoys all the trappings of financial success: penthouse apartment, a foreign sports car, a summer home in the most fashionable vacation community. He is handsome and bright and physically fit. "But I feel flat," he told us at our meeting. "My biggest regret is that I'm not enjoying what I suppose should be the best years of my life. I'm not even thirty and I have more than my father ever dreamed of having his entire life. What more can I possibly want? And yet I'm constantly dissatisfied.

"Actually, I don't want more of anything," he hurried to add. "This isn't a story of greed. It's more a question of feeling sort of disappointed and unfocused."

Cy is not alone in his inability to enjoy his dramatically rapid achievements. *More and more young adults who have soared to the heights of their professions find that the rarefied air at the top is disappointingly thin.*

There are many possible reasons for the regrets of early success. One established explanation is the notion that life's meaning lies in the journey, not in the harbor. George Bernard Shaw offered another, typically acerbic view: "There are two sources of unhappiness in life. One is not getting what you want; the other is getting it."

The intriguing paradox of early success is that we can actually wind up distrusting our powers rather than feeling confident about them. F. Scott Fitzgerald's first novel was published when he was only twenty-four years old, to great acclaim. Reflecting on that period some twenty years later, when his life had turned considerably bleaker, he wrote, "The dream had been early realized and the realization carried with it a certain bonus and a certain burden. Premature success gives one an almost mystical conception of destiny as opposed to willpower. . . . The man who arrives young believes that . . . his star is shining."

As Fitzgerald suggests, without being careful to balance fate's gifts with more prosaic qualities—willpower, careful planning, and hard work—the starry skies of early success may be followed by some very dark mornings. Drunk on our own heady powers, we can dissipate much of our promise in the false belief that our talents are invincible. If there should then be even a moderate fall from grace, it seems as though our destiny has been suddenly and irrevocably reversed.

We don't have to be artistic prodigies to experience a plunge in self-confidence or feelings of helplessness when our luck turns. "I simply overextended myself," says Barry, his voice heavy with self-blame. At thirty-four, he had recently gone into bankruptcy, after having operated a very successful computer store for three years. "I borrowed a great deal of money because the business looked so promising, but as it turned out, it wasn't enough money to cover the growing expenses of an expanded operation.

"I just didn't realize that I couldn't offer the kind of services I was providing and still make enough profit to keep going. At the same time, the slowing economy kept my customers from paying me on time, and I couldn't raise any more capital to make up the slack. Regret? I'm filled with it. Because I made stupid choices out of the belief that enthusiasm and high-quality service would be all I needed to make my business successful."

When Barry's friends tell him that at his age he can certainly begin again, he waves them off. "I want to believe that, but I feel now that my success *was* just luck. I keep meeting guys who began businesses about the same time I did who managed to stay afloat and now are bigger than ever. No, it's over for me. I had my chance and I blew it."

Barry is feeling far more regretful than his experience calls for. Clearly, he can't hold himself responsible for a lowered economy, nor should he underestimate how difficult it always is to launch a new business. On the other hand, he isn't using regret's potential as a valuable source of self-learning. Instead of allowing self-blame to cause a total withdrawal from further business ventures, he might try to assess how his tendency to be idealistic and impulsive affects his decision making. Seeing his mistakes as a valuable tool for positive change rather than as a painful source of self-hate would also lessen his envy and competitiveness with more successful colleagues. If he stopped viewing their success as terrible reminders of his own inadequacy, they could actually become a valuable source of advice and guidance for Barry in the crucial early stages of some other business plan.

What is especially distinctive about Barry's story of feeling like a has-been, when he is barely into his thirties, is that it reflects the obsession with youth and power that so dominated society during the 1970s and '80s, the years of Barry's adolescence and early adulthood. Clearly, he came from an era that didn't view early success as atypical. The cultural messages that shaped Barry's behavior still push us into the race for money, power, prestige, and fame at a remarkably early age—as if *not* to have satisfied every aim of adult life by the time we hit thirty is really the aberration.

Now, in the early years of a new decade, there are signs that at least some people are reexamining these values. Two major reports in *The New York Times* and *Time* magazine, both based on large-scale research samples, indicate that people in their late teens and early twenties are trying to resist cultural pressure to make their mark quickly. They are deliberately taking longer to commit themselves to either permanent relationships or careers.

What worries some older observers about this shift is that the new generation of young adults may also be resisting growing up and taking on what we have always considered to be adult responsibilities. Others feel, however, that such slowing down is a positive attempt to strike a better balance between individual needs and cultural expectations. In a demographic study of young men and women, economist Martha Farnsworth Riche disputed the criticism that these young people were simply drifting aimlessly, refusing to make any choices about their lives. "They are making choices," she insisted. "But given the changes in the world around them, they can't make definite choices at the same age people did before."

The trend toward slowing down does seem encouraging, because it suggests that people may be trying to examine how they really feel and what they truly want before making choices and taking action. As another report in *Time* magazine noted, people are "thinking hard about what really matters in their lives." The rather deliberate pace also seems more in line with current theories of development in young adulthood.

Although our culture seems to deny it, the transition into adulthood is not an overnight process; it is gradual and highly complex. Daniel Levinson, a pioneer in the research into adult development, believes that some fifteen years are needed to leave adolescence, find our niche in adult society, and make the commitment to a more stable way of adult life. According to Levinson, this transformation does not take place until around thirty, often closer to thirty-three.

In our twenties, although there are so many decisions to make, our decisions cannot always be carefully considered because we are still forging, not finished with creating an adult identity.

While we may believe that the twenties are a time to build empires, in reality they are a time to test the waters, try out options, explore possibilities. What's more, if at thirty these earlier choices no longer seem satisfying, our desire for new options is also in many ways a quite natural process. Certainly we should try to avoid making impulsive changes in our previous life structure, but even if our failures are of grand proportions, it helps assuage regret to understand that *failures are a legitimate part of the experimentation of the first phase of adult life.*

As we move out of our twenties, we make new attempts to find true adult direction. We realize that while we may have thought we knew what the "right" choices were for us in our twenties, our conception of "right" was still greatly defined by external forces: what our parents wanted for us, what other

authority figures told us was important, what the culture
sanctifies, and what our idealized image of ourselves drove us
to achieve.

What's more, we often sweep into our twenties still carrying the adolescent illusion that we can do almost anything
we set our minds to. Liberated from the restrictions of childhood, at the beginning of autonomous life, we are particularly
susceptible to society's assurance that now nothing is beyond
our eager, hungry grasp. Not surprising then, that in our thirties we can begin to experience the intense regret that comes
with realizing that our illusions led to some choices that really
didn't express our truest goals and values.

One recent survey of young adult women illustrated this
difference in perception between the twenties and thirties.
Women in their twenties tended to view the world much more
optimistically than did the older women, who had already observed how omnipotent fantasies erode with real-life experience. The younger women felt they could easily combine
marriage, career, and children, whereas most women who had
already tried to integrate these roles cited definite drawbacks
to either their children, their marriages, or their careers.

Young men and women share many of the challenges—
and burdens—of contemporary choice. As we saw with gender differences in childhood, however, women's experience
seems to create particular kinds of regret, especially in the area
of balancing personal and professional roles. Continuing social inequity can embitter many women over thirty, who regret being doubly duped by the idea that "you can have it
all."

Like her male counterpart, a woman has to deal with the
inevitable realization that, in fact, life is a series of concessions
and trade-offs. However, she also discovers that she stands to
lose much more, even in the 1990s, than a man does. It is still
much easier for a man to succeed professionally and have a
family life. Ninety percent of male executives under forty are

fathers, but only thirty-five percent of women executives under forty manage to build a career and have children.

Even before they are faced with the dilemma of children
versus careers, women, who are conditioned to place a high
value on attachment to others, will struggle with the battle of
self-versus-other when it comes to such issues as a couple's
concurrent career demands.

Sarah, a thirty-six-year-old department store buyer, had
just landed a job with her city's premier store when her long-
time boyfriend, Max, was offered a prestigious engineering
job in Seattle. Although they had put off plans for marriage,
Sarah believed there was a good chance that they would indeed one day make the relationship a permanent one. "But I
didn't think it would happen if I didn't agree to go along with
him. I didn't think we could withstand so much distance in
our relationship at that point."

With considerable apprehension about stepping off her
current career ladder, Sarah made the move to Seattle with
Max. A year later they were married, and she was working at
an increasingly satisfying job when Max was transferred again—
ironically, back to their home city. Max was willing to work
out a commuting arrangement, but it was quite clear that he
felt they should really be together. Sarah contacted her former
boss, and while his second offer was not quite as good as the
first, he did want her back.

"And so now," Sarah told us, "I'm back here with Max,
in a job that I can't complain about but that isn't nearly as
exciting or clearly promising as my old job. I keep thinking of
what I gave up in leaving in the first place, then what I lost
in leaving the job I'd started in Seattle, and now what I'm
losing by working but not really attaching myself to the new
job, because I know that for the next few years, Max is going
to continue moving around. But it's hard to really figure out
my losses, because my relationship with Max is truly getting
better and better."

In this period of her life particularly, it's wise of Sarah to
deal with her regret over a disjointed career by concentrating

on the gain of a strengthening marriage rather than on her professional losses. It's estimated that somewhere between one half and two thirds of women who were married in the 1980s will divorce. While career conflict is not the villain in the story of modern marriage, it is certainly often a contributing factor to tension. Because a good relationship with Max is truly important to her, it is a genuine choice for Sarah to put her marriage ahead of her career right now.

Some women might feel angry at finding themselves in Sarah's situation, but her priorities are such that she is comfortable with her decisions, particularly since she is planning to make up for her losses later on. Max has promised that at a given time in his career he will reciprocate Sarah's sacrifice by putting her professional needs ahead of his own.

"I have to try to keep remembering that, given the circumstances of loving a man whose job depends on his mobility, in many ways I have the best of both worlds. It's not everything I wanted, but for now it's enough." As Sarah suggests, *sorting out our values is a way of balancing the ideal with the practical so that we can accept something short of the ideal without suffering excessive regret.*

Male or female, successful or still struggling to succeed, we begin to question what we are doing and why we are doing it as we move into our thirties. We become more reflective, and wonder what deeper goal we might have given up to be the person we seem to have become. We can turn again to Georgia O'Keeffe, who was twenty-nine years old before she realized that she was still allowing voices other than her own to guide her choices.

"I grew up pretty much as everybody else grows up and one day . . . found myself saying to myself—I can't live where I want to—I can't go where I want to—I can't do what I want to do—I can't say what I want to. Schools and things that painters have taught me even keep me from painting as I want to. I decided I was a very stupid fool not to at least paint as I wanted to and say what I wanted to when I painted, as that seems to be the only thing I do that didn't concern anybody but myself."

O'Keeffe's epiphany at the age of twenty-nine illustrates the kind of conflict we often go through when, as we get older, our own voices become more insistent. We begin to reassess the place to which choices made or neglected in our twenties have brought us. For example, young women and men talked to us over and over again about wishing they had not given up on early aspirations to paint, or act, or write, or dance.

Anita is a math teacher in her late thirties. "I get a lot of positive feedback in my job, both from my colleagues and, even better, from my students, but it doesn't dim the awful regret I carry around for having given up the study of voice. I loved opera passionately," she told us, "and I was really quite gifted. I was given genuine encouragement by some of the finest teachers. But the older I got, the less enthused my parents were about my interest in music. They wanted me to use my skill in math and science to get into a stable profession like teaching. When it was time to go to college, I let myself be talked into a school that had a great math and science department, even though it had very little to offer in the arts, particularly in voice training. My parents were sure I could find some private studio near the college to keep up with my singing.

"Well, they were wrong. I couldn't locate any outside studio that could really develop my talent, and I had all I could do to keep up with the heavy demands of being a math major. I stopped studying music altogether. Even though I should have known better, I told myself I could pick up singing again later on. But later I had to face the fact that voice study isn't like writing a novel that you can go back to after a hiatus. You need to always practice and keep up your technique."

Anita acknowledges that she might not have been successful as an opera singer, considering the extreme competitiveness of the field, but the intensity of her regret stems from never having tried to make it happen. What's more, she says with inescapable sadness, "I can't even enjoy being part of an opera audience. All my life, opera has been the guaranteed antidote to any despair. The minute I sat down at the opera or a voice recital, I forgot all my problems. Now, the pastime that gives me the greatest pleasure is taken from me because I feel such a terrible sense of loss and deprivation."

In fact, no one has "taken" this pleasure from Anita's life but Anita herself. If she honestly examined her sweeping rejection of music, she might discover that vanity and envy play a part in her inability to be involved with singing in any way but as a star. Painful as this realization might be, it could help her see that while her missed opportunity will probably always be a regret, her current attitude is greatly contributing to the feeling's intensity. If she can change her rigid attitude that being onstage is the only way to have music in her life, she could possibly recapture the comfort she always found in being part of an active audience.

The regret over choosing the clearly charted road instead of the less certain path has always been an element of the artistic life. Artist Robert Henri continually urged his students to decide what was personally important early on, to sort out their own values and follow the road that might lead to creative fulfillment. "If I were you," he told them, "I would prefer a short and courageous career . . . to one that would be prolonged by hedging. What does it matter if by standing for the thing you really believe in, fighting for it . . . making no weak concessions, you fail? Such failure is success. You keep your likeness, anyhow."

While Henri's point is important, in order to avoid the bitterness of failure, it is also important to be realistic about our talents and about how much we're willing to sacrifice to achieve our goals. For example, students often asked Joseph Campbell whether they should attempt to launch difficult careers as painters or writers. Although he is famous for his advice to "follow your bliss," he answered that they should think about whether they could endure the loneliness or disappointment that might lie ahead. Only if they thought they could continue pursuing their dreams without counting on ar-tistic success in the foreseeable future did he encourage them to go ahead.

It is also helpful—when deciding whether to pursue a dream or, perhaps more important, leave it behind—to con-sider how we can integrate it in new ways into our lives. For example, instead of passively mourning her lost dream of op-era, not only could Anita remain part of a devoted audience, she might continue studying as an accomplished amateur, or even teach singing on some semiprofessional level.

As we move into our thirties, we have begun to challenge a perception left over from childhood that may have influ-enced some other early choices that we now regret. This im-mature perception, explains psychiatrist Roger Gould, is that there will always be someone to lean on for support, someone to rescue us from failure. If we were influenced by this feeling when we formed an earlier important relationship, we may have searched out a caretaker rather than an equal partner.

Many people who marry in their early twenties are ac-tually looking for a "disguised parent." As a result, they may feel some considerable regret over the marriage five or ten years later, when they have evolved further into adult life. There is the disquieting sense that they should have gotten to know themselves better before making such a serious, long-term commitment. Gould observes that the feeling "I wish my mate would accept me for what I am as a person" takes a sharp upward turn between the ages of twenty-eight and thirty-two, while there is decreasing agreement that "For me, marriage has been a good thing."

Philip, thirty-four, married Jane when he started medical school. Now, already quite successful in his specialty, he is questioning not only the quality of his marriage, but why it ever took place.

"I feel so ungrateful," he said with some frustration. "Don't think I don't know all the statistics about doctors who dump the wives who put them through medical school. Well, at least I don't have to feel guilty about that. My parents paid most of the bills, and I got a good bit of scholarship money.

"But I'm just not enjoying our marriage. . . . It's like it doesn't speak to *me* . . . only me as Jane's unchanging husband. She's a wonderful, nurturing woman, but I feel I don't need that kind of relationship now, and yet it seems to be the only one that makes her comfortable.

"I know it sounds horrible, but I realize that when we married, I was terrified of facing medical school, and I buoyed myself up by doing something really grown-up: getting married. (But of course I chose a maternal woman who would make me feel perfectly safe while I was pretending to be so mature!)

"Now, though, I really do feel as self-reliant as I pretended I did then, and I have much more confidence. So I'm feeling incredibly regretful that I closed off so many possibilities for myself before I knew who I really was. Or at least who I was on my way to becoming."

In many ways Philip feels as if he is falling apart, and indeed, that's exactly what he is doing. His old self is disintegrating, making way for the new, more fully formed adult. The temporary sense of dislocation as he makes this shift can certainly be enormously disorienting. The big questions Philip faces in this time of transition are whether his marriage can accommodate his new vision of his life, and whether he is willing to make the effort to see if it can.

Such decisions are especially troublesome today. As in other areas of experience, there are diverse moral guidelines for staying in an unsatisfying relationship, especially one made at a time you have quite literally outgrown. Unlike earlier times, when we valued commitment over choice, self-sacrifice over self-fulfillment, and social good over individual pleasure, we can be tempted to choose our own needs over those of a person we still care for and respect.

Yet, as Erik Erikson and others note, *being able to maintain our own identity while sharing intimacy with another person and preserving our own sense of self in the relationship is the major issue in young adulthood.* It is also the particular challenge of contemporary love and marriage. Philip decided to handle the challenge, and his conflict, by persuading his wife to go with him for counseling and by making a promise to himself that he would stop dwelling on the "mistake" of marrying too early. He has also accepted the validity of his own changed needs. If, after a reasonable period, the marriage does not grow more vital, he will ask for a divorce. "Of course I'll feel guilty about it, but I've decided that self-sacrifice is not the most productive way to resolve my guilt."

Unlike those who regret marrying early, some people find (often to their own surprise) that as they enter their thirties they regret still being single. "Last summer I went to a wedding just about every other weekend," says James. "Next birthday, I'll be thirty-five, and I'm beginning to feel some regret about not having a family under way. I have to admit, though," he added, sounding a little embarrassed, "that I also really enjoyed the bachelor existence. I may sound very superficial, but I liked the randomness of the relationships, the concentration on uncomplicated pleasures."

What James discloses is hardly surprising, in light of the cultural emphasis on freedom that seems to encourage people to delay settling down. However, if James had evaluated his choices from a less narrowly focused perspective, he might have felt differently about giving up the "uncomplicated pleasures" of his bachelorhood. This more broadly focused way of seeing is what Harvard philosopher Robert Nozick describes as a "zoom lens ability."

Just as a zoom lens on a camera moves in and out to afford various perspectives on a scene, it is possible to look at the landscape of our own lives with an attention that moves "back and forth from the general picture to details, from confirmation to things that don't fit, from the surface to what is deep, from the immediate to the long-term." Although the focus of our attention is always shaped by who we are, we will also in turn be shaped by what we see. As Nozick explains, "Over the long run, a person is molded by where his or her attention continually dwells."

While James was caught up in playing the part of the freewheeling bachelor, his focus was set only on the exciting moment, the undemanding relationship, on being promiscuous and uncommitted. Consequently, he paid too much attention to this image of himself and too little attention to uncovering more buried and perhaps more potentially rewarding images of what he could be, such as a caring husband and father.

The sense that we might have waited too long to make certain choices can also touch our professional lives. Here again we see a paradox of modern life, and an explanation for much of its regret. On one hand, we're encouraged to live like adults before we are developmentally ready; on the other hand, we are also encouraged to think of ourselves as being as free and unconstrained as children.

At thirty-six, Martin has had a number of more *and* less successful attempts at a variety of careers. A talented graphic artist, he had no desire to work at a large "establishment" advertising agency. Instead, he chose free-lance work, for clients who generally had more creativity than cash. When he was single he greatly enjoyed his freedom, and although it wasn't always easy, he managed, with occasional help from his parents, to make ends meet.

"But then I met Barbara," he explained, "and she teaches nursery school, a career she enjoys a lot and is really gifted at. But of course it's not a field where she's ever going to make a lot of money. We wanted to marry—she's my age, and isn't happy about waiting too long to have children—and I suddenly felt ready, or at least willing, to take on a more traditional career. The trouble was, when I started looking for work, all I could get were entry-level jobs for which I was ridiculously overqualified."

The casual commitment Martin made to his career, which he found so satisfying in his twenties, now haunts his thirties.

"I'm not regretting that I didn't compromise myself over the years," he told us, "but I do regret not having made more money and establishing a more solid place for myself professionally."

Martin's previous lack of self-consciousness about his professional achievement is beginning to shift over into anger and self-deprecation. He wishes he'd struck a better balance between freedom and professional forethought and that he'd used his talents more judiciously. In his twenties Martin understandably wanted to experiment with a more flexible career, but by not shaping his vocation more actively, by not balancing experimentation with planning, he took a basically passive, childlike approach to work. He was hanging on to an immature fantasy that at some point something would happen, or some disguised parent would come along to transform his assorted career experiences into something substantial.

Separating from the fantasy of parental salvation has still another connection to the tasks of young adulthood. This is a period when we try to create a wider psychological distance between ourselves and our parents. We are trying to become—and to feel—sufficiently self-reliant and competent to take our independent place in the real world. As we take this place more firmly as adults, we are often inspired to examine our childhood relationships with new candor and courage.

Twenty-five-year-old Betsy is the daughter of a famous writer who recently died. In a news-making divorce trial he had won custody of Betsy and her sister when the girls were three and five years old. "We were never allowed to see our mother after that, and he filled us with stories about her selfishness and wildness. He was in many ways a devoted parent, but I now realize that I lived fully by his view of the world, which always had him in the much revered center.

"After he died, my sister and I went through his papers and found some incredibly arrogant diary entries that made it clear that taking us from my mother was far more a way of

punishing her for leaving him than for our best interests. At
that point of discovery, I felt a great pull to find my mother,
and now we're trying to make up for the time we lost. I'm
grateful we've had a second chance, but I'm enraged at my
father's selfishness. I know this may sound horrible, but I regret most of all that he'll never know the degree of my anger,
that he died still thinking I worshipped him."

Accepting the reality of her father's selfishness and giving
up the fantasy of his perfection constitute an important step
for Betsy in developing what Daniel Levinson calls "an adult
consciousness." She will move even further toward this desirable state of consciousness when she is able to see her father
in all his complexity. Perhaps in her thirties, she will be able
to measure him in less black-and-white terms, and integrate
the picture of him as a vindictive, self-absorbed man with that
of a devoted, attentive father.

Overall, *the major question in young adulthood is how to make
good choices out of a confusing array of possibilities and personal
desires.* To answer this question more successfully, we can turn
to a very effective decision-making technique. When faced with
important choices, we need to weigh possible losses against
expected gains. As we do this we are in effect practicing what
psychologists Irving Janis and Martin Mann call "anticipatory
regret," anticipating the losses inherent in each possible choice.

We often engage in this process automatically, as we run
down the possible outcomes of a major decision. *Deliberately*
using this crucial technique will allow us to assess objectively
both our possible gains and losses from a particular action and,
perhaps even more important, how we will feel about these
results.

As we rehearse the various scenarios that might emerge
from a choice, we can clarify some core issues that play a part
in our response. *We can consider our potential gains and losses in
two sets of possible repercussions:*

First, what we may gain or lose by making the choice.
And, will we feel better or worse about ourselves
    afterward?

Second, what others close to us can gain or lose from
    our taking the action.
And, will other people see us more or less favorably?

In taking this inventory of anticipated regret, we are
pausing for a healthy moment and trying to question what
hidden pitfalls may lie behind even the most tempting option.
As novelist Milan Kundera wrote, "A question is like a knife
that slices through the stage backdrop and gives us a look at
what lies hidden behind it."

Philip, the man deciding what to do about his marriage,
was employing anticipatory regret when he ran through the
possible outcomes of either trying to revitalize the marriage or
ending it quickly to make the most of a new start. He could
see that if he summarily ended the marriage, while he would
be free, he would lose as well as hurt a woman whom he still
genuinely cared about; he would disrupt his children's lives;
in years to come, particularly if his relationship with his children suffered, he might regret having been so self-centered;
and he would certainly suffer criticism from friends and family for being so ungrateful for his wife's sacrifices. Determin-
ing to seek marital counseling before asking for a divorce was
the direct result of using the guidelines of anticipatory regret
to shape important decisions.

Too often, if we are not consciously employing anticipatory regret, while we may believe we've considered all the
possible consequences of a decision, we end the deliberation
too quickly.

Tony, at forty-eight, looks back with increasing regret at
a decision he made when he was thirty-eight. At the time, he
and his wife had two children very close in age, and both
births had necessitated Caesarean deliveries. "We both felt,

after our second child was born, that two healthy kids were enough.

"Because of the Caesareans, Kathy and I agreed that she shouldn't have to submit to another round of surgery to have her tubes tied, and birth control devices were a drag and not one hundred percent reliable. It seemed like a sensible solution for me to have a vasectomy.

"No one in my family has ever been divorced, and it never occurred to me that my marriage wasn't for life. How could I have known then that eight years later we'd be divorced and the kids would be living with her three hundred miles away? To tell you the truth," Tony says, shaking his head, "I still can't believe it."

Recently, Tony met a woman whom he feels he would like to marry sometime soon. But she's never had children, and since she's in her thirties, she wants to have a child fairly soon. Tony is planning an attempt to have his vasectomy medically reversed. "But," he says unhappily, "even though she's told me she'll marry me whether or not we can have children, I worry about what will happen if the vasectomy can't be reversed."

Since Tony is nearing the decade mark after which vasectomies become much harder to alter, his anxiety is legitimate and deepens his regret over his early, somewhat impetuous choice.

"I felt at the time that I might regret the vasectomy later, but on the surface and at the moment it seemed right. I just didn't think seriously about the long-range consequences. If I had, I might have decided to put up with the hassle of birth control and giving up some spontaneity in our sex lives rather than taking such a drastic measure. I didn't know any guys who had ever had a vasectomy, so there really wasn't anyone I could talk to about the decision except for my wife and the urologist, who both just saw it as a reasonable thing to do."

It would have been useful to Tony to have tried harder to find some objective counsel and talk through his dilemma before making his decision. Taking the time to gather information and seek meaningful advice is always an important step in anticipating the consequences of our decisions, but never more so than when the risks are not immediately apparent. With friends, family members, and colleagues we respect, or in the absence of these, perhaps a therapist or counselor, our perspective can be broadened so that we have a fuller picture of the hidden risks and drawbacks to the decision we feel so pressed to make now.

Helpful as it is to think ahead in this way, however, there are occasional hazards to this decision-making process. At the one end, we can get stuck in a state of procrastination and dwell endlessly on our possible losses, afraid not just to make the "wrong" choice, but ever to make a move at all. (Like T. S. Eliot's J. Alfred Prufrock, we become suspended in our own inertia, with "Time yet for a hundred indecisions, / And for a hundred visions and revisions.") On the other end is the temptation to puncture the anxiety aroused by the process of anticipating regret by making impulsive decisions.

Exceptions aside, however, if used carefully, anticipatory regret can be helpful at any stage of life. Still, it is a particularly meaningful tool in early adulthood, because we *are* forced to make decisions that will have lasting impact on our lives while our values and priorities are still in flux. The process can bring us closer to recognizing our emerging mature self— even if that self seems so changing and elusive.

> "Who are *you?*" said the Caterpillar. . . .
> Alice replied, rather shyly, "I—I hardly know, sir, just at present—at least I know who I *was* when I got up this morning, but I think I must have been changed several times since then."

If only there were a perfect moment in the book,
if only we could live in that moment,
we could begin the book again
as if we had not written it,
as if we were not in it.

—MARK STRAND, "The Story of Our Lives"

SEVEN

Regret and Middle Age

If any one characteristic can be said to capture the regrets of the years between forty and sixty (the middle chapters in this book of our lives) it would be reassessment: of the dreams and goals with which our story began, and the actions we took (or didn't take) in their pursuit.

What have I done with my life so far, and why have I done it? What do I get from my wife, my husband, my children, my friends, my work, myself? What do I give to the people I care about? Have I used my talents and abilities well? Is there still time to use them or to use them differently? Have I wasted too many years to recapture an early dream? Do I still have those dreams, or have they changed? Have they changed because I truly lost interest, or because I was afraid to admit how deeply I cared?

Such appraisal of our lives in middle age inevitably heightens an awareness of youth's passing; and our sense of loss can awaken other losses, particularly the bittersweet memories of early love. The theme of unforgettable encoun-

ters with love's first ecstasy and passion has lured generations
of poets. Lord Byron, for example, writes:

> If I should meet thee
> After long years,
> How should I greet thee?—
> With silence and tears.

And former poet laureate Galway Kinnell remembers:

> In a tiny room
> overlooking a bridge and a dark river
> a dim
> past-light
> hovers over a narrow bed
> where a girl and a boy give themselves
> into time, and memory, which affirms time,
> lights their moment
> all the way to the end of memory.

The wistful longing for love that slipped away can even
invade a life that is reasonably fulfilled; for probably more than
any other area of life, we tend to mourn and often idealize
relationships that never blossomed into full fruition.

"Every time I hear French spoken, I remember my first
love affair during my junior year in Paris," says Nancy, a successful editor. "He was a French architecture student, and when
the semester ended he begged me to stay on in France. I desperately wanted to, but I was afraid of what my parents would
say, and of interrupting my education. It's twenty years since
I've seen Claude, and I consider my marriage more than successful, but I still can't go to a French movie without getting
misty-eyed.

"There are times when, even though I know it's crazy, I
feel that I miss things like the romance of Paris in the rain,
and nights in cafés, drinking wine straight from the vineyard.
It's an intensity of passion that I know you can't build a last-

ing relationship on and that has to do primarily with beginnings. But sometimes when I feel so 'middle-aged,' I think how wonderful it would be to have that exquisite feeling of love in its first explosive birth again."

In fact, many men and women do find new and even first love in midlife. Yet we often believe that romantic intensity—along with a whole range of other experiences—is no longer possible now that we are no longer young. In his research into adult development, psychiatrist Roger Gould discovered that as adults reach fifty, there is often a clear decrease of what was once a powerful conviction: that there is still plenty of time to do most of the things we want to do. As we begin to measure our lives not by how many years we've lived but by how many years we have left to live, we wonder whether there truly is still time to develop new skills or fulfill at least some of our long-delayed wishes or fantasies.

There is also a newly felt poignancy to choosing between those middle-age options that are still possible. Weighing one choice over another in midlife, we are operating with what sociologist Alice Rossi calls a different "time calculus: if I do X, will I ever get to do Y?" We are conscious that the option we give up in preference to another may be lost to us forever. Each choice taken or rejected now carries the disconcerting weight of a potential "last chance."

Virginia Woolf, in *The Waves*, describes this acute midlife awareness: "As I drop asleep at night it strikes me sometimes with a pang that I shall never see savages in Tahiti spearing fish by the light of a blazing cresset, or a lion spring in the jungle, or a naked man eating raw flesh. Nor shall I learn Russian or read the Vedas. . . . But as I think, truth has come nearer."

As Virginia Woolf suggests, disturbing as the middle-age time calculus can seem, our confrontation with it is a crucial aspect of our continuing development, and our ability to deal with the deepest truths of our lives, including the truth of regret. Compared to the person we were in life's earlier chapters, we are increasingly able now to be self-aware and introspective, to think about what really matters in our lives. Poised at life's midpoint, we can begin a crucial reconciliation among what is, what was, what might have been, and what still may be.

Coming to terms with the meaning and truth of our life is the challenge and achievable hallmark of middle age.

At one time, childhood and old age were seen as the only stages of life in which people changed significantly. In childhood, the changes were positive: We grew and developed; our lives expanded. In old age our physical powers declined, and the scope of life narrowed. In between these two periods of great flux, one was simply an adult: a stable, fully developed man or woman who accepted the existing social values of commitment to family and community, and played roles appropriate to this traditional code. There was usually little impetus to question whether your adult role was personally satisfying.

Contrary to that limited (if perhaps less anxiety-producing) scenario, midlife is now recognized as a period when change is much more the standard than stability, and when questions about contentment and significance abound. Since we are now able to see the choices and experiences that brought us to this point, we have a heightened understanding of poet Andrew Marvell's often quoted line "Had we but world enough, and time," and we vow to make the very best use of the precious time that still lies ahead.

Honestly confronting our past, and learning from our "mistakes," we can begin now to use our regrets for constructive change in the future: *to rethink earlier decisions, to take new action and rectify where possible, and—perhaps the most constructive response of all—to begin to make peace with the irreversible decisions and missed opportunities of our personal history.*

The regrets of midlife touch every aspect of our experience. Not surprisingly, given our culture's emphasis on professional success, *middle-age regret often focuses on education and careers.* In our teens and twenties we spin wonderful dreams of mastery in a variety of fields. Choosing the right one will surely lead to a lifetime of achievement. Since we rarely contemplate time's running out, we can show a cheerful lack of concern about putting other choices aside. After all, they can always be taken up again later.

Our thirties bring us closer to modifying our dreams, but we still have a sense of real opportunity and possibility. Now in our forties and fifties, we long to recapture that earlier sense of limitless time. Facing the middle-age truth that some of the options we hoped to return to may never be realized can make career disappointments especially painful, often awakening regrets over not having taken our education more seriously.

A major regret of people in middle age is not having worked harder at school to shape their future careers better. Interestingly, this regret is not only experienced by people whose career advancement was curtailed by a lack of quality education; it also plagues men and women who went to the best colleges and have gone on to achieve considerable success.

"I look at these young kids with their papers published in major scientific journals before they even turn thirty, and I'm green with envy," says Dennis, who at forty-eight is the managing director of a major pharmaceutical company. "I probably earn more in a year than they'll earn in ten doing pure research, but I find myself wishing I had really applied myself harder when I was in college and graduate school. I've got money and power and prestige, but most of the time I'm bored to death. Maybe if I'd really tried to apply myself to study back then—seen myself as a scientist rather than a person who could parlay a science background into a good living—I would have gone on to experience some of the excitement this kind of person seems to feel about his work."

In fact, more than ever before, it is possible today for people to compensate for such regrets. Dennis could easily join the population of older students returning to school, which has reached a national all-time high. Whether he chooses to return to graduate school to formally pursue a Ph.D. degree so that he can one day teach and do research, or simply take courses in science to update his knowledge and rekindle his old excitement about learning, he does not have to feel that intellectual excitement is lost to him forever.

A major reason why so many middle-aged people are drawn to further their educations is that the stirring of boredom in a job we mastered long ago, or frustration over not pursuing a career we might have preferred, will peak at this time of life. In part, this is because these are the years when our *professional* lives peak. According to sociologist David Karp, many people who have risen to the height of their professions by their forties and fifties feel "topped out. They know where they'll be for the rest of their occupational lives."

For people who find certainty monotonous rather than comforting, a new sense of urgency will haunt midlife issues of achievement and job satisfaction. Too goal-oriented to realize it on the way up, some people are unnerved to discover that success may not compensate for work that doesn't feel meaningful. Others who find work reasonably enjoyable may feel an urge to develop a part of themselves they've previously neglected. However, while more and more middle-aged people are making changes in their professional lives, Roger Gould explains that many men and women in midlife still believe that "it's too late to make any major changes in my career."

"I became seriously depressed in my job at forty-five," Bryant, now fifty-three, said, describing his career as a high school social studies teacher. "I had liked my work well enough in the beginning, but when I hit my forties I began to be miserable. I wrestled with the decision to strike out in a different direction, like getting a master's degree in counseling because the kids really seem to like talking to me, but I couldn't get past my fear of losing the security teaching provided.

"The years between forty-five and fifty were really the pits. I was angry at myself and just about everyone else. . . . I don't know how my marriage survived my relentless negativism about my work. Finally, at fifty, I made a decision to take early retirement at fifty-five."

The decision, he discovered, was a major breakthrough in living with his regret. "It was really quite amazing. I found I was suddenly able to put new energy into my work, to be more creative with the kids, and to my surprise, they responded. I'm really grateful to be closing out my career this way, instead of with feelings of resentment. I realize now that deciding to retire helped me feel I was finally taking some control of my life. I'd been so mad at myself for not having had the courage to leave teaching. Being willing to risk giving up the benefits of staying on until conventional retirement age made me feel at least a little braver and allowed me to give up that agonizing litany of 'if only.' "

T. S. Eliot's J. Alfred Prufrock reflects in middle age:

> And indeed there will be time
> To wonder, "Do I dare?" and, "Do I dare?"

Clearly, Bryant's regrets over being what he considered cowardly in his forties have been greatly eased by daring to take risks in his fifties. "In fact," he says, "maybe if I didn't have so many regrets about my forties, I wouldn't have found the courage to move on." Bryant is now exploring all sorts of ideas for life after retirement. "I may even go back to school for that counseling degree, or join the Peace Corps, or even do volunteer work in a shelter for runaways. It's all enormously exciting. However," he adds carefully, "don't take this to mean I still don't deeply regret having stayed with teaching. My advice to people in their forties who are unhappy with their jobs—no matter what their profession—is to get out while you still can, do something else if you really need to, even if it means a risk and less money. Otherwise you risk something much more dangerous . . . spending the rest of your life with a building sense of waste and anger at yourself."

Men and women in midlife who share Bryant's unhappiness with careers that have ceased to satisfy them can avail themselves of a number of part-time educational or independent study programs that make preparing for a second career much more feasible. In fact, a constructive use of regret would be to research aggressively how to ready ourselves for a more challenging vocation while realistically examining how such changes might affect our lives. As we set the wheels of change in motion, we should also be compassionate toward the fear that threatens to keep us rooted in the unsatisfying but safe status quo. Understanding that the fear of change is as old as time, we can buoy ourselves up with further advice from the eminent painter Robert Henri: "Never let the fact that things are not made for you, that conditions are not as they should be, stop you. You must go on anyway. Everything depends on those who go on anyway."

Unlike Bryant, who taught for many years before admitting that he regretted his vocational choice, Gwen, another teacher, knew almost immediately that the educational bureaucracy stifled any hope she had of finding fulfillment in a teaching career. However, she, too, has used the broader perspective of middle age to find peace in her career.

"On a bad day I still wonder why I did go into teaching, and berate myself for staying with it. But now that I've reached my forties, I have to acknowledge that if I had really wanted to change careers, I would have done so a long time ago. Obviously, I found compensations, and now I'm trying to admit to them and concentrate on them so I can let go of my regret on this score."

It is almost always possible to find ways of enriching our careers. In midlife we owe it to ourselves to abandon self-pity and passivity and take the initiative in energizing our work. "I've begun to take an active hand in improving on the job's intellectual challenges, instead of bitching about its limitations," says Gwen. "I consult on textbooks. I help write curricula. I create special programs for gifted students."

Gwen also feels better about her still somewhat unsatisfying career because she has realistically evaluated her life's priorities. "My big leap in letting go of my regrets," she says, "is that I've decided it's okay for your career not to be so rewarding if you don't make it the center of your life. My personal relationships and my leisure activities, like travel, have always been enormously important to me, and teaching gave me the freedom to devote real time to both. So, in a way, while I would love to feel excited about my work, I can appreciate its value in the overall scheme of my life."

In middle age we are more able to let go of some regrets because we see them in a broader perspective. We are also better able to persevere even when other regrets continue to darken our lives. Indeed, if poet Robert Frost captured the dilemma of choice in young adulthood when he wrote, "Two roads diverged into the yellow wood, / and sorry I could not travel both," Dante sums up midlife when he says in *The Inferno:* "In the middle of the journey of our life I came to myself within a dark wood where the straight way was lost. Ah! How hard a thing it is to tell what a wild and rough and stubborn wood that was."

Regret will darken midlife most of all when we remain confused about what goals are still possible to achieve. We can feel that change is impossible or, at the very least, painfully slow. Providing we have the courage to examine our lives, are willing to face facts, and accept the irreversible, significant, and even astonishing change can occur in middle age.

By the time we reach our forties, one thing we have certainly learned is that along with joy, life brings periods of suffering and disappointment. Trying to accept and integrate these inevitable feelings into our lives can mediate self-blame for past decisions. *Honest but nonjudgmental reflection on our past can also help us take a newly active role in building a more personally meaningful future.*

Social psychologists Bernice Neugarten and Nancy Datan studied a large group of middle-aged people and found themselves immensely "impressed . . . with reflection as a striking characteristic of the mental life of middle-aged persons: the stocktaking, the heightened introspection, the conscious processing of new information in the light of what one has already learned, and the turning of one's proficiency to the achievement of desired ends. . . . These people feel that they effectively manipulate their social environments . . . and that they create many of their own rules and norms."

"Every once in a while I wonder, 'Did I do the right thing— was it really *that* bad?' And I say, 'Yes! I did, and it was!' " Cynthia tells us with a smile. Cynthia, a statuesque forty-six-year-old, is dean at a small liberal arts college. She had only recently left a childless twenty-two-year marriage to a husband suffering from what she called "terminal infidelity."

Despite some counseling and a short separation early in their marriage, she had continued to endure a relationship that gave her little joy, and which assaulted her self-esteem. Although she always wanted to be a mother, her biggest regret is not that she didn't try harder to have children. "He didn't really want children, and when I realized it was going to be difficult for us to conceive, I just let time slip by rather than take medical steps to try to correct the problem. Perhaps realizing when I passed forty that time had made the decision for us accelerated my resentment, not to speak of my disgust at my own passivity.

"As I've gone over and over my past, however, I've finally almost forgiven myself for my role in not having children. Because I think that if I did have children, I probably wouldn't have been able to pursue my career in the same way, and then I might never have found the courage to leave a marriage that no child could truly benefit from."

Cynthia explained that a move up the career ladder had given her the self-confidence to feel she could really take care of herself . . . "that I could risk the unknown of divorce to get out of a bad situation, but I certainly wish I'd done it when I was younger. Divorce has turned out to be the most exciting adventure I've ever had," Cynthia now declares. "I feel really in control, after being so passive and controlled for so long."

Bernice Neugarten and Nancy Datan call this kind of proudly autonomous response "the executive processes of personality in middle age," in which we feel a heightened, or even totally new, perception that we can take charge of our own experience.

We can try to awaken this sense of personal command by consciously working to overcome the image of ourselves as helpless and dependent. In daily life, for example, we can practice being more assertive in situations as minor as returning spoiled food to a store; in protesting being interrupted while having the floor at a neighborhood meeting; in demanding respect from a family member or colleague. Each chip in the restraining wall of passive dependence adds to our courage in risking autonomous behavior.

As we let go of our feelings of powerlessness, we will find avenues of self-expression and mastery that we would never have thought possible, and certainly never believed could *begin* in midlife. "A few months ago I saw an ad in the paper for sailing lessons," Cynthia reports with a wide, infectious grin. "I've been a pretty athletic person, but I'd never sailed. Yet something compelled me to sign up for the class. I absolutely loved it, and made two very good friends among the other women in the class. Then, as luck would have it, our instructor decided to move to California and wanted to sell her sailboat. So we three women pooled our money and bought it! And every chance we get, we take it out. Sailing is a spiritual and physical escape, but I especially love the idea that I can handle a boat, handle the elements . . . things that would once have totally intimidated me."

Unlike Cynthia, many women still cannot move out of their conditioned sense of dependency, staying tied to relationships that are at best unrewarding, and which are often seriously destructive. Year after year passes without their gaining the confidence to challenge their sense of inadequacy and risk facing the unknown. In midlife, however, they are often finally pressed to do so.

Sheila is a woman still trapped by her feelings of helplessness, although she is struggling to escape from them. She acknowledges that she has stayed in her marriage more out of passivity and fear than from having made a real choice. It is an admission that greatly intensifies her regret: *We most often regret those choices we make out of fear and insecurity, for they are, in fact, not choices at all, but only desperate attempts at finding security.*

"My husband is basically a good man, I suppose," Sheila says, "but he's totally insensitive to my needs. While I was raising the children—and I pretty much was left to do it all myself—I was able to push down my dissatisfaction with him. But now that we're alone together, resentment just keeps bubbling up inside me.

"Most of all now, though, I fault myself for being so submissive in the past. Maybe if I had been different, he would have been different. It was a good marriage when we started out. I desperately want to change my life now, but either route to change scares me: trying to fix my marriage, or finding the courage to leave it. What scares me very much is how hurt and angry I am, now that I'm really admitting all my regrets about the past twenty-two years. Whether I leave him or stay, how am I going to be able to forget all this built-up pain?"

In fact, to move ahead with her life, Sheila shouldn't try to "forget" her pain, but rather to accept it as part of her personal history, for only by accepting it can she begin to gain control of the bitterness that is now eroding her life. *Accepting the pain of regret is preferable to "forgetting," because acceptance implies some resolution within ourselves, rather than an unconstructive attempt at denial.*

Sheila has to face the fact that whatever she does with the rest of her life, many memories of her marriage will always be painful. Even if she tries to rebuild her marriage, she will never recapture the years of lost intimacy.

We cannot rewrite the past; we can only try to control our attitudes and feelings about it. Acceptance of our miscalculations and mistaken decisions will not necessarily make us feel better about what we did, but we can, in time, move toward some measure of compassion for the regretted behavior.

Compassion for herself will bring Sheila closer to the possibility of forgiving her husband for the bitterness and loss she feels. When we've been hurt, many of us vow to "forget but never forgive." In fact, it is only the opposite idea that allows us to repair damaged relationships. In deciding to forgive her husband, Sheila would be letting go of the anger that inhibits personal growth and the possibility of making constructive change. To forgive, even while holding on to the painful lessons learned, is not an act of submission. Rather, wrote philosopher Hannah Arendt, "Forgiveness is the key to action and freedom."

Another major midlife regret stems from our cultural preoccupation with staying young. It is often a considerable shock to experience signs of physical decline, whether it's being less agile when we swing out of bed in the morning, or suddenly needing reading glasses after a lifetime of 20/20 vision.

Joseph Campbell explained how his study of myths showed that "the problem in middle life, when the body has reached its climax of power and begins to decline, is to identify yourself not with the body . . . but with the consciousness of which it is a vehicle." Psychologist Bernice Neugarten also observed that in midlife our attention and values shift from the physical to a "sense of interiority," with primary emphasis on our "intellectual and spiritual life, rather than on our physical attributes and prowess."

These observations are psychologically valid and important, yet we all know that modern values proclaim something quite different. You are only as good as your hard body and wrinkle-free face. Never mind that you've passed your fortieth or even fiftieth birthday; never mind your achievements or intellectual accomplishments. How you look (meaning how young you look) is often the principal measure of self-worth.

"I go to the gym with these magnificent women, some of them not much younger than I am, but of course many much, much, younger, and I feel it's ridiculous to think that if I leave Paul, I'll ever find another relationship," Sheila told us. And an attorney named Ken, at forty-five, is involved in yet another of a series of relationships with beautiful "girls" half his age. (Predictably, he met his new girlfriend at the gym, where he works out frantically every night of the week.) He seems to feel that by having young lovers he can halt the passage of time. In fact, the normal regrets one feels about aging are greatly intensified if we continue to value ourselves primarily by how youthful we manage to look.

We *are* developmentally ready in middle age to face up to our own mortality and to the mortality of those we love. We are ready to give up our childish need for safety, and the search for what Roger Gould calls "magical solutions" to aging and death. While taking care of our bodies and taking advantage of cosmetic surgery are reasonable routes toward feeling and looking better, we should be sensitive to whether they only serve to deny the reality—and inevitability—of our own aging process. For down that road, toward the impossible goal of *being* young, lies only the bitterest regret.

Middle age is actually a time when, if we make the effort, we can find remarkable compensations for youth's passing.

The desperate self-consciousness of youth is frequently replaced by an exciting disregard for other people's opinions or a need for their approval. We know our strengths and much more calmly accept our limitations. We know what pleases us and are far less afraid to ask for it, or even to demand it, such as insisting on a mate treating us with respect, or a boss not being abusive.

In midlife, we are not only much less driven by our impulses, we are much more able to affirm the impulses that express our authentic selves. As psychiatrist Roger Gould says, *in our late forties and fifties we find a place in the world that is finally defined by our own values and goals rather than those held by other people.*

*   *   *

"It seems like the older you get, the fewer regrets you have," says Jay, "because priorities change, and some things aren't so important as they were—like other people's opinions."

"Yeah. When I was younger I used to be curious about how everyone else was living," his partner, Simon, added, with an engaging laugh. "Now that I know, I don't particularly care. I've found what's right for me."

Jay, fifty-one, and Simon, fifty-three, are a gay couple who have lived together for more than ten years. Each had struggled separately with his sexual preferences while maintaining traditional marriages and a similarly frustrating pretense of heterosexuality.

For Jay, the decision in midlife to end his marriage virtually meant losing his children, as his wife won full custody and then promptly moved across the country. Jay seems to feel remarkably comfortable with this clearly painful consequence of his actions.

"I deeply regret having lost my kids for those years, having missed part of their childhood, but now that they're old enough to make up their own minds about me, they've started opening up some lines of contact despite their mother's attempts to keep them away.

"When I left them, it was because I was approaching forty, and I knew I had to look at what I would eventually regret more, once they were grown . . . continuing to live a life of utter denial or admitting that I was gay and risk losing my children's respect, and maybe their place in my life forever.

"Perhaps it was selfish, but I chose to leave while I still had a chance to build a good relationship with someone I loved for the rest of my life. And I truly came to believe that staying in the marriage would have embittered me so much that I wouldn't have continued to be a good parent anyway."

Nonetheless, he admitted, during the first year or so before he met Simon, "I was overwhelmed with great waves of self-hate. But to be honest, the older I get, the less regret I

feel about what I did. I've always provided for the kids financially, so I can't blame myself on that score. Who knows? Maybe
I'm just better able to accept that in fact I *am* selfish. I may not
be the self-sacrificing parent I once fancied I would become.

"While I certainly continue to wish it could have happened with less pain to people I truly do love," he finished
thoughtfully, "I know in my heart I did what I had to do at a
time when I finally felt capable of taking the risk."

Shifting to a discussion of why he waited so long to come
to terms with his sexual preference, Jay's reasoning echoed
that of many homosexuals who also did not reveal their sexuality until they found the courage of midlife:

"Yes, of course I regret that it took so long for me to be
open about my sexuality, but I simply couldn't then. Other people's opinions were too important to me. My perspective about
what is important is completely turned around now. After
I hit my forties I decided only I can know what's right for me."

Jay's lover, Simon, also left his children, and he accepts
their resentment as the price he has paid for the right to live
authentically.

"I deeply regret the chaos my 'coming out' caused them.
I also wish I had been able to do it earlier, when they were
still babies and less conscious of the implications of my choice.
But I simply wasn't ready to take that step until I hit the wa-
tershed of getting near midlife. The times I was part of, my
social status, the fact that I was practicing law in my community, and my fears of what it would mean to my own parents
to have me acknowledge my homosexuality kept me underground until finally I was ready."

"Being ready" is a major factor in midlife's resolution of
regret. Whether being ready involves leaving a job or a marriage, having a love affair or admitting to repressed sexuality,
in midlife we are newly able to take on experiences that we
would probably have anxiously run from ten years earlier.

"Once I realized that, in fact, I hadn't been ready earlier,
I stopped regretting the time I wasted before 'coming out,' "
says Simon. "The fact is, in an ideal world I would have ex-

pressed my sexual needs early on. In reality, I needed to be at the stage of life I was in, not to just have the experience but to admit its importance."

Youthful notions of what the adult good life is supposed to be form an integral part of Simon and Jay's long years of denial, and their related regrets over wasted time. As we attempt to assess the past in midlife, we discover how many of our choices have been shaped by illusions and assumptions we weren't able to shake, even though they appear to have little to do with our real needs and desires.

Psychiatrist Daniel Levinson believes that midlife is a time when we are able to come to grips with these youthful illusions, and also to recognize that many of our conditioned beliefs are simply invalid. He calls this process "de-illusionment" and distinguishes it from "disillusionment," which causes us to lose our deepest beliefs and grow cynical. Levinson explains that "de-illusionment" brings both relief and disappointment, freedom and a sense of loss. He adds that if we continue to cling to old illusions about what will make us happy, we will fall victim to an unhappy corollary: If we don't reach our goals, "life will be a total failure and have no value."

Still another major source of regret in middle age relates to our success or failure as parents. Psychiatrist Roger Gould confirms that when people reach their forties, "there is a sharp rise in the stabbing regrets brought on by 'my mistakes in raising my children.' " The stress of being a parent is intense, and when we look back from the vantage point of midlife's sense of greater mastery and self-understanding, it can seem that we were too overprotective or overly critical, too absorbed in our careers or our own personal needs, too demanding or unforgiving. We can desperately wish for the chance to change our behavior and undo the damage.

In fact, the now familiar sight of a middle-aged man, clearly enraptured with the baby he pushes along in a stroller, with his young new wife at his side, illustrates a popular new role for the successful man who regrets how little pleasure he took in parenting his first set of children. Whether or not we create new families, we can ease the regrets of past parenting by being better parents to our grown children. This may take the form of being more open to their criticism of us, both past and present, and to work on modifying certain attitudes that continue to interfere with our relationship.

For some parents, disappointment and self-blame lie in our children's falling short of our fantasies for their lives (and for our own achievements as parents). As Rabbi Harlan Wechsler asks, "What parent doesn't feel, when he looks at his child and sees what he doesn't like, that he has failed?"

"My son graduated from Harvard with a Ph.D. in classics and made a halfhearted attempt to find a teaching position," says Lucy, shaking her head in dismay. "Now he's living at home, working as a waiter, earning just enough to pay for his daily expenses—there's never a mention of paying us rent— and he seems in no hurry at all to leave the nest or make more focused plans. I had such dreams of the pride I would feel at accomplished grown kids. . . . It's a bitter disappointment, and I can't help but blame myself for wasting so much potential. I think back to how truly unaware as a person I was when he was small, and I realize I made an awful lot of mistakes in terms of shaping his goals and motivations."

Other parents have difficulty resolving regret over their loss of parental power now that their children are grown and gone. "My daughter is in a terrible marriage," says a middle-aged father, "and I know it's only going to end in grief, but there's nothing I can do about it. I tried to stop her from marrying that creep, but she went ahead anyway. Now she's paying a terrible price, and I feel horribly impotent. I can't stop feeling I should be able to relieve her pain, and I wish I could at least let go of the pain I'm so overcome with myself every time I think about her."

Parental self-blame is not, of course, a solution to the problems of grown children. We must use midlife's improved perspective to accept what cannot be changed in our children and to forgive ourselves for what we may or may not have done wrong as parents. We must also remember that children have an innate sense of self that defines their lives quite apart from our influence as their parents.

Coming to terms with family dynamics is equally important for the middle-aged child. As we look at our aging parents or mourn their death, we may have a tendency to berate ourselves for not having been better sons and daughters, visited them more often, taken more active care of them when they were ill. We can never be completely the child or parent we would like to be, if for no other reason than that the story of family life is one that bears the mark of many authors as it travels through the generations. Psychiatrist Theodore Isaac Rubin sums it up nicely: "We are all the victims of victims, and this fact must be accepted if we are to be realistically compassionate with ourselves, *our* parents, and our children."

Some of the regrets of parenthood—as well as regret over never having been a parent—can be eased in middle age by developing our *potential for generativity.* Erik Erikson, in his brilliant study of Gandhi, describes how in middle age the leader was able to create "for himself and for many others new choices and new cares."

According to Erikson, middle age is primarily fueled by the response he calls "generativity." As we become less self-absorbed, our own new choices and cares are more directed toward helping make a better world for future generations.

In order to achieve a sense of generativity, says Erikson, "a man and a woman must have defined for themselves what and whom they have come to care for, what they care to do well, and how they plan to take care of what they have started and created." Drawing on our broadened vision and accumulated experience, we can begin to refine our personal legacy to the world. We may become a mentor to younger people and colleagues, willingly sharing talents, interests, or skills that we might once have kept competitively to ourselves. We may use our skills to participate in a teaching program, or do volunteer work, or work actively for social change.

Men in midlife can sometimes be quite surprised by their impulses of generativity, as well as by their sudden desire for emotionality and intimacy. In fact, this is the time when a kind of yin/yang process takes shape, when men develop their feminine side and women their masculine side, integrating the halves into a newly enriching whole.

"I've experienced what feels like an abrupt change in my feelings about family life and friendship," says Cliff, a highly successful executive. "I have enormous regrets about how arid my emotional life has been all these years. I always pushed my sons to head tenaciously for a business career, but now I'm telling them to ease off, to look at other aspects of life as well. I tell them they better be very careful how they prepare for their professional lives—because I've learned that what you concentrate most of your energies on is what you end up with. I reached a point where I could run any meeting or solve any business problem, but I was absolutely incapable of sharing even that pathetically small piece of inner life I was able to get in touch with."

Conversely, women in midlife who are free to develop their masculine side find great excitement in feeling newly self-absorbed. Freud's granddaughter, Sophie Freud Lowenstein, believes that many women, including herself, are able to be more courageous, assertive, and aggressive in midlife because they can finally let go of the lessons first learned as little girls, the need to play out the traditional role of nurturer and care-taker, and the value of being connected to others.

Dr. Lowenstein says that she did not feel a true sense of individual identity until middle age, after having gone from being "the best-behaved little girl in Vienna," to being a de-voted wife and "perfect" parent, to being a dedicated social worker. At that point, first overcoming the guilt she felt over a "selfish choice" to return to school to seek a new career, she became a college professor. In teaching she found work that truly fulfilled her, and that allowed her to express generativity in a new and creative way.

A woman's passionate career commitment in midlife can

"When Julia and I talk of becoming old, we always end by agreeing that one has to take a position on it. One has to prepare, ahead of time, an image of oneself that can be lived with."

—GAIL GODWIN
A Southern Family

EIGHT

Beyond Regret: Late Adulthood

It is never too late to live creatively. Michelangelo lived to nearly ninety, and was painting almost to his last breath. Verdi wrote *Falstaff* at eighty. Between the age of seventy-eight and his death at eighty-four Richard Strauss composed ten new concertos, sonatas, and songs. Musical scholar Mosco Carner comments on how these later works by the Romantic composer showed a new "classical tendency . . . greatly enriched and mellowed by the artistic and human experience of a lifetime." Similarly, although Brahms's compositions were always complex, his very last composition was a set of Chorale Preludes for the organ that, according to most critics, were especially notable for their deepened sense of tranquillity and introspection.

In fact, Erik Erikson says that it is extremely important to nurture creativity in later life. Many older people, he found, expressed "profound regret at having relinquished such activities as painting, singing, playing music and photography."

While talents peak for many people in youth, there is a provable "resurgence of creativity" in old age. Harvey Lehman, in a study entitled "Age and Achievement," points out that the most important paintings in the Louvre were painted by artists in their thirties—and in their seventies. His examination of lyric poetry showed a level of excellence among poets between twenty-five and twenty-nine, and another high when they entered their eighties.

Psychiatrist Anthony Storr reminds us that these creative shifts have always been part of the artistic life, provided the artists lived into old age. "When men and women of genius live long enough," he says, "changes in style become so apparent that it is customary to divide their work into periods . . . 'early,' 'middle,' and 'late.' " Storr found a particular characteristic of the late period to be a quest for personal understanding rather than winning public praise. Consequently, this third-period mindset often resulted in work that was quite unconventional, unifying elements that might once have seemed completely incompatible.

Philosophers also appeared to be exceptionally productive in their thirties, but were equally thoughtful and productive long past eighty. Frederick Franck is an artist who began his career in medicine and dentistry and then in middle age turned to his real passion, philosophy, in which, at nearly eighty, he remains deeply involved. He passionately believes that being actively engaged with life and learning and self-expression is essential to a rich old age. "I may not run as fast as I once did, but I am not tired. Or, rather, when tired of writing, I start to draw. When tired of drawing, I play my piano."

"I remember my youth and the feeling that will never come back anymore—that feeling that I could last forever, outlast the sea, the earth, and all men." In Joseph Conrad's memory of youth's sense of surging immortality, we find poignant contrast to the older person's intense awareness that, unlike the sea and earth, there is a limit to our existence.

Life expectancy continues to increase, but once we pass our sixtieth birthdays, *forever* becomes a word of vastly diminished scale, no matter how carefully we tend our aging bodies. The fact that death is no longer an abstract or romantic concept limits our pleasures on bad days and, on bad nights, can crowd our room with visions of a lamented past.

One way that people have traditionally coped with this new awareness is through a sense of spirituality. Many of us have strayed from the religious training of our youth, but in late life we may quite consciously try to find new sustenance in continuing our spiritual development.

"I was such a good Catholic girl," Annette, sixty-seven, said.

"And later, all the time I was married and the kids were young, I tried to adhere to some kind of religious practice, though doubts kept bothering me. I managed to get the kids through first Communion and confirmation, but as I got into my forties, and my marriage broke up, I felt more and more removed from Mass and other rituals. I still felt a personal relationship to God, but even that waned after a while. It got to the point that I became one of those 'lapsed Catholics' you hear about all the time now. But since I've gotten older, something started shifting again. I found myself searching for some sense of religion to ease some of my confusions about what my life means. I'm still not a devoutly religious person, but I do go to church and I'm finding more solace in rediscovering my faith."

Age and death are popular themes of secular as well as religious literature, but in a book about choice and regret there is probably no more relevant issue than the one expressed in Jack London's vow: "I shall not waste my days trying to prolong them. I shall use my time."

Clearly, *a key to making the most of this last stage of life is to move beyond the regrets of our lives so far.* This does not mean denying regret's accumulated sorrow but, rather, incorporating regret into the total picture of our lives. If we can accept the mistakes of each earlier stage of development—not using youth's energy to do some of the things we really wanted, not seizing opportunities before we lost them, not making the most of a relationship—we will suffer less regret from what Erikson sees as old age's potential for despair.

"In old age," Erikson explains, "when it's too late for restitution, coping with ancient 'wrongdoing' can add poignantly to the lurking if not pervading sense of despair." Old age prompts us to measure what we have, to reflect on what no longer is, and to accept or anguish over what has never been. Despair can hover over such life assessment, for our attempts to cope with the past once and for all can usher in what Erikson calls the "pervasive triad: Guilt. Remorse. And . . . Regret." These three feelings are linked together in old age, because we are trying now to bring the still unresolved past into some state of resolution. With our knowledge that we have very little time left to correct past mistakes, regret deepens over not having better used our one turn around life. Yet, although despair is a natural component of this stage of life, its presence can be significantly contained.

Acknowledging the influence of past, present, and future can lead to a successful integration of all our experience, including our regrets, into our lives as older people. Self-compassion and self-acceptance can bring a rewarding sense of well-being from believing that our lives had and continue to have meaning. While we may certainly still wish we had more time, "in such final consolidation," says Erik Erikson, "death loses its sting."

Trying to make peace with the life lived thus far is a normal process of old age. Gerontologist Robert Butler sees this thoughtful looking-back process, which he refers to as a "life-review," as a necessary part of adult development, helping us find some measure of peace in late adulthood. Indeed, he believes that a successful life-review can bring us greater peace and a stronger sense of self than we have ever known before.

Writer Saul Bellow vividly captures this attempt to make peace with our lives, in his novel *Herzog*. The title character is suddenly "overcome by the need to explain, to have it out, to justify, to put in perspective, to clarify, to make amends. . . . He sometimes imagined he was an industry that manufactured personal history, and saw himself from birth to death."

Herzog's life-review is not reassuring. He comes to a highly disturbing conclusion:

> Considering his entire life he realized that he had mismanaged everything—everything. He went on taking stock, lying face down on the sofa. Was he a clever man or an idiot? Well . . . he might once have had the makings of a clever character, but he had chosen to be dreamy instead, and the sharpies cleaned him out. He was obliged to admit now that he was not much of a professor, either. He had made a brilliant start in his Ph.D. thesis. . . . But the rest of his ambitious projects had dried up, one after another. He had been a bad husband—twice. To his son and his daughter he was a loving but bad father. To his own parents, he had been an ungrateful child. To his country, an indifferent citizen. To his brother and sister, affectionate but remote. With his friends, an egotist. With love, lazy. With brightness, dull. With power, passive. With his own soul, evasive.

For Robert McNamara, the Secretary of Defense during the turbulent early years of the Vietnam War, the life-review was disturbingly complex, for his actions then affected not just his own but our nation's history. He told a writer for *Time* magazine that he had come to realize, "because of misinformation and misperceptions, there are misjudgments as to where a nation's interests lie and what can be accomplished." The war did not have to grow to the proportions it did, he saw, looking back. The casualties of the war, both spiritual and physical, could have been greatly reduced.

The Secretary also wondered whether his wife's death was influenced by the war, and her husband's role in it. "She was with me on occasions when people said I had blood on my hands."

As he continued his reflection on his personal life, McNamara expressed the belief that his inner self remained hidden from other people, even most likely from his own children. "And let me tell you that's a weakness. If you're not known emotionally to people, it means you haven't really communicated fully. . . . I know it's a weakness of mine."

Robert Butler explains that we also see the life-review in people of any age who, because of accident or illness, are prematurely facing death. Another political figure, Lee Atwater, chairman of the Republican National Committee during the presidential campaign of 1988, in 1991 was suffering from a malignant brain tumor at the age of thirty-nine. With life clearly waning, he also felt the need to reassess his life, and to confess his professional and personal regrets in a national magazine.

Describing in the article for *Life* magazine how he currently struggled many nights against the fear that "I will never wake up again," he apologized for the "naked cruelty" of his remarks about Michael Dukakis, who ran against the Republican candidate, George Bush.

"Fighting Dukakis, I said that I'd . . . 'make Willie Horton his running mate.' " (Horton, a black man, raped a white woman and murdered her husband during a weekend pass from a Massachusetts prison. Atwater's strategy was to imply that Dukakis was too much of a liberal to protect the citizenry.)

As he continued the review of his life, Atwater divulged other regrets. He recalled how badly he had treated the chair-

man of the Democratic National Committee after the victo-
rious Republican election.

"When I would run into Ron Brown, I would say hello
and then pass him off to one of my aides. . . . Since my illness, Ron has been enormously kind . . . and I have learned
a lesson. Politics and human relationships are separate. I may
disagree with Ron Brown's message, but I can love him as a
man."

New York Times columnist Anna Quindlen writes about
the poignant lessons of these public confessions: "The regrets
of two men, one aging, the other dying . . . regrets as corro-
sive as Mr. Atwater's disease, as sad as Mr. McNamara's eyes—
about what we did in the world, about who we are at home,
two things that are inseparable . . ."

Although less dramatically, and with less sweeping implications, our own history unfolds before us when we are
old, and we all become audiences to our lives, observing, reflecting on the significance of various experiences, reevaluat-
ing people and events, summing up what we did, what we
didn't do, what we wish we had done or wish we hadn't done
meanly or wrong.

Robert Butler points out that younger people can help the
older person cope with the developmental challenges of old
age by allowing such reminiscing to take place without growing impatient or mistaking it for senile ramblings. Indeed, it
can be enriching to the listener to participate in a process that
all of us will one day encounter in ourselves.

It is understandable to wish in old age that we could have
another chance—and to be overcome with sadness that it's no
longer possible—to make the kinds of decisions that would
have enriched our later lives. However, if our life-review goes
well, the landscape of age will seem much brighter. We may
even find that life has been given new meaning through age's
heightened capacity for self-awareness.

As we replay our past experiences, it's as if we had found
an old letter or diary. All of a sudden we can see ourselves as
young people, pouring out feelings that burst to be expressed,

but which then were lost in time. Not only are we suddenly able to remember those feelings, but with the greater wisdom of age, we can more fully understand the young man or woman who sounded so sad, defensive, angry, or compliant. And because we do understand, we are often able to forgive the foolish or even destructive choices that our feelings may have influenced. This dramatic level of self-reconciliation is expressed in the Chinese vocabulary by a phrase, *hui zhi bu ji,* which translates as "It's too late for regret." The ultimate promise of the heightened insight and deepened compassion of old age is that *in this last stage of life, we can finally be beyond regret.*

Old age will not contain serenity, however, if we don't start working toward that inner peace earlier in life. We are often reluctant to look into the future and try to imagine what it will feel like to be old. As B. F. Skinner pointed out, "Everyone wants to live a long time, but no one wants to be old—or to think about being old."

It is our observation that if any planning for old age does take place, it invariably concentrates on trying to ensure that we will be physically well and financially secure. We jog and exercise and give up alcohol and cigarettes; we hire investment counselors and pay strict attention to corporate retirement policies. Let others die a premature death or worry about money in old age because of inefficient planning—we'll have no regrets on that score.

But what about making the kinds of choices that will allow us to take pleasure in the years we've planned for so practically? In large part this means trying to get as much pleasure as possible from our lives while we are still young. When they looked back on their lives, many older people we spoke to told us they wished they had been able to live more fully in the moment when the moment was at hand.

There had often been, they saw now, a vague but tenacious sense that they weren't entitled—yet—to make the choice of pleasure over duty or responsibility. During our career building and caretaking years, even allowing ourselves small rewards can seem frivolous or selfishly time-consuming. *Later,* we tell ourselves earnestly—when we retire, or at least when many of our responsibilities have abated—will be the legitimate time to enjoy the fruits of our lifetime of labors.

"We both worked full-time and had four children and then, in the last ten years of her life, also cared for Bob's mother in our home," says Edith, seventy-two years old. "We'd get in bed at night exhausted, and we'd put ourselves to sleep by spinning dreams of what we'd do someday when we finally got the time and extra money to relax and be responsible only to each other and ourselves. It just didn't occur to us that by the time that happened, maybe time wouldn't be so plentiful.

"Three years ago Bob's mother died, and our children finally seemed to have their lives reasonably together, and so we decided, okay, when Bob turns seventy, we'll both retire. And we did," she says firmly, a smile of memory lighting her face. "Our first extended vacation was heavenly. We couldn't get over the feeling of freedom, of spontaneity, of not having to think of someone else before making any decisions.

"Six months later, Bob dropped dead of a cerebral hemorrhage. All that saving for the future, and where did it get us? Yes, I have a healthy nest egg, but I'm an old lady living alone. How I wish that we'd allowed ourselves to enjoy life together earlier!"

Clearly, we need to examine, before we reach old age, whether we are fixing our gaze on the future with a steadfastness that obliterates the present. To prevent ourselves from being haunted by regrets of wasted relationships—including the relationship with our deepest selves—we need to live now, whenever and wherever now is. We need to nourish ourselves with a quality of life that doesn't rest only on the possibility of future rewards.

"Putting our life on hold for the future was a dreadful idea," Edith continued softly. "I comfort myself with the knowledge that overall we didn't have an unhappy life. My regrets are not even for my sacrifices to others, although I'm sure other people would think some were goody-goody excessive. It's simply that Bob and I waited too long to do many things that were personally important.

"And of course we underestimated the role that health and fate would play in our old age. Bob was such a stickler for sensible living—I guess I thought he'd go on forever. But even if he had lived longer,"she finished thoughtfully, "we still expected too much to happen at the end of our lives. If I had to do it over, I'd insist that we build some more into life as we went along living it."

One thing that Edith might do to ease her sadness about not living her life more fully with her husband is to try to develop stronger relationships with her now nearly middle-aged children. This is a stage of life in which we can dispel some of midlife's parenting disappointments by coming together in newly satisfying ways.

"The best time to enjoy a child is right away, no matter what his age is," says a grinning Mort, seventy-four. As he flipped through a photograph album, he happily reflected on the recent summer travels captured in each snapshot. "I had to make caretaking arrangements for my ailing sister in Ireland," he explained, "and I decided to ask Mort junior to come along—he was nearly forty at the time—so that he could get a taste of his origins. We never did anything together when he was young. I was too busy and he was just as busy with his own life. Even then, he was a nut about photography. He was really surprised when I raised the idea. . . . I think he thought I was joking, but then he got excited at the prospect of being able to photograph Ireland, because it isn't the kind of photography he does professionally.

"Even though he has the money himself, I insisted on making it my fortieth birthday present to him. I wanted the pleasure of giving him something he'd really enjoy and remember after I was gone. And it was great. We were a little awkward with each other at first, because we'd never spent close time together like that, but it got better and better. I wish I had done things like that when he and I were both younger, but 'better late than never.' And it seems like it's really made a big difference between us.

"So many times I think about that trip, how many memories my son and I share now. Can you believe that it still pops up in our conversation every time he calls or visits? And he visits often," he said proudly, reminding us for the third time how successful his son is as a photographer.

Mort obviously feels greatly satisfied at his closeness to his son. Often, there is a practical edge to fostering closeness with a grown child that has to do with the regret we feel over the physical losses of old age.

Writer Malcolm Cowley suggests that a good relationship with adult children helps parents cope with the losses of aging. "Accept, accept is the rule," Cowley advises about old age's increasing dependence. "Let younger persons exult in their strong arms and their . . . eagerness to be helpful."

It is difficult for many older parents to accept the changes in some caretaking aspects of their relationships with their children. It feels "wrong" to be more on the receiving end of help and concern. In fact, such a shift is in many ways the natural evolution of the parent-child bond, and we can take some comfort and pride in having a child who is genuinely interested in our welfare. If we aren't self-conscious about losing some of our own powers, we might find real joy in allowing the strong arms of adult sons, daughters, and even sons- and daughters-in-law to support us emotionally and physically.

As we saw with Mort, it is never too late to try to deepen the connection between our children and ourselves. But, even if that connection still seems difficult, grandparenthood can be a way to move beyond our parenting regrets in a singularly constructive fashion. In a study of aging, Joan and Erik Erikson, along with Janet Kivnick, explained, "The pleasure that grandparents can take in the accomplishments and growth of their grandchildren can go a long way to help resolve past issues over caring for and parenting their own children." They point out that grandparenthood offers us "a second chance at generativity."

A grandchild is often the indisputable bridge over a troubled relationship with a grown son or daughter. In part this explains why, for many people, becoming a grandparent is such a powerful experience, often to their own surprise. "I feel that my grandchildren are giving me a second chance at mothering," says Lois, sixty-eight. "I'm so much less ambivalent than I was with my own kids, so much less conflicted. And I'm so much more able to just be *present* . . . to delight in their growth and accomplishments. I know my kids are probably surprised at how good a grandparent I've turned out to be, and I think it's helped them be more forgiving about some of the blunders I made when they were young."

Indeed, the intensified goodwill of grandparenthood gave Lois the courage—and the generosity—to invite her daughter to explore their regrets over the past.

"One afternoon, when I had successfully deflected my ten-year-old granddaughter's temper tantrum, I looked up to see my daughter staring at me with a rather wistful look on her face," Lois remembered. "I was sure I had a good sense of what she was thinking . . . how punitive I used to get when she expressed anger to me when she was a child. So, something just told me to talk about the disparity . . . and to try to explain that the reason I was so demanding then was primarily due to my sense of inadequacy as a mother.

"It was enormously liberating to admit my regrets about my mothering," Lois said, her eyes suddenly filling with tears. "It was terribly scary and painful, but then I encouraged my daughter to tell me what she remembered feeling about our relationship while she was growing up. I think she really believes now, despite the many resentments she revealed, that I wish it could have been otherwise, wish I could have prevented some of her hurt. Maybe more important though, and this is what I mean by a second chance, I think she knows that I'm expressing my love for her when I reach out to her child."

Today's child, in particular, can also reap major benefits

from this grandparenting bond. Psychotherapists are very familiar with patients for whom a grandparent's love and acceptance provided a lifesaving oasis in bleak, even abusive childhoods. Also, living as we do in a time when divorce is so prevalent, grandparents can offer grandchildren an important refuge during a period of parental conflict. We can also grow closer to our own divorced children by actively giving the kind of help that's needed to cope with single parenthood.

So, whether or not our children forgive all the mistakes we once made in raising them, we *can* begin to forgive ourselves. *Forgiving ourselves may, in fact, be life's final and most important challenge.*

Some of the behavior most difficult to forgive ourselves for is careless squandering of physical fitness and stamina. Lung cancer and emphysema, the payoff of years of smoking, and heart attacks following a lifetime of rich eating and drinking, can make old age dismal and emotionally and physically burdensome. We should try to alter our destructive behavior early enough in life so that these final years aren't filled with unnecessary suffering.

If poor health diminishes happiness in old age, satisfaction and self-acceptance contribute to physical health and a sense of well-being in older people. There is always an intriguing subjectivity to appraising how good we feel. If we are doing well at something, or feeling particularly loved, our tolerance is much higher for pain and discomfort. Never is this premise truer than in old age.

After a major investigation into what makes people happy, psychologist Michael Argyle discovered a close relationship between health and contentment. "Some people complain about more pains . . . than doctors can find a basis for. Others are less concerned about their state of health than their doctors are . . . and, among people with the same level of health, as assessed by their doctors, those who are unhappy or nervous feel that they are in worse physical shape."

Argyle observed that one major factor in people who feel happy—and consequently physically healthier—was their ability to change a situation that disturbed them, or, conversely, their increased attempts to adapt better to circumstances they could not change. "I forget all my aches and pains when I'm at my tool bench," Michael, eighty-one, told us happily. "I really fought against moving to this retirement community . . . it felt like going out to pasture. But then I realized that, considering the state of my health, which was certainly not going to get any better, I really had no choice but to live in a more sheltered environment. I'm taken care of here . . . people watch out for me.

"Then I decided to do something really new, that I had never done before, to make myself feel some excitement about life, less like I was just filling up time. And it's really worked. Now I'm even taking on commissions from other residents, making a bookcase or a coffee table, and I may even start giving a small class to a group. It's a great feeling. My body may be deteriorating, but my brain still feels young and strong."

Samuel Beckett said that when we grow old, we have to be ready to "Try again, fail again, fail better." An interesting phenomenon of aging is that not only do we "fail better"—with more compassion for our mistakes—sometimes it seems better to have failed.

Maryann, sixty-six, an energetic executive, told us that she had many fewer regrets as an older person than she had when she was young. "Your outlook shifts—things that seemed important in earlier years are not necessarily important later. In fact, earlier regrets can no longer be regrets at all, and some can even become assets."

We listened carefully as Maryann explained: "In my thirties I had an affair with a married man and became pregnant. He wanted me to have an abortion and told me if I didn't, he would have nothing to do with the child—or with me. I felt a complete fool and a failure, but because of my age I went ahead with the pregnancy. I wasn't sure that I would ever have the chance to have a child in a conventional manner.

"Having my daughter outside of marriage in those days resulted in my living a life relatively outside of a traditional framework, which I certainly had never thought I wanted to do. For years it really troubled me terribly: I felt regret about depriving my daughter of a 'normal' life-style. But as the years went by, not only did she and I develop a wonderfully strong bond, but at different phases of my life I enjoyed two long and wonderful relationships with men who for different reasons I made the choice not to marry. I felt strong enough as a separate person to feel I didn't have to marry someone unless I genuinely wanted to be with him for the rest of my life.

"Now that I look over my life, I feel that both my daughter and I have benefited from what I once considered a dreadfully foolhardy choice. She has a great sense of her own independence—modeled, I like to believe, after my own—and I think this greatly compensates for the security she might have found in a more conventional upbringing."

Marvin's experience with regret has come to a similar point of closure. When he was fifty he decided to leave his high-powered job for more exciting opportunities with an investment firm. "That was fourteen years ago. I wasn't with the new firm long enough to enjoy my impressive office, let alone my inflated salary, before the company got into trouble over some reckless investments, and along with about forty other people, I was laid off. Even then I didn't get too upset, because I was pretty full of myself and was sure that with my background, I'd have no problem finding something else equally splendid.

"But to my chagrin, and amazement, the jobs just didn't come along. Finally, to keep my family from starving, I took a job in the development office of this small college where I am now. Even after all these years and several raises, the pay is only a third of what I earned fifteen years ago."

All during his fifties, Marvin told us, he obsessively regretted having made the first move that started his "decline." "I kept kicking myself for being so reckless. And my self-

esteem was completely shot. Every time I sat in this little office, with so little happening, I felt I had thrown my life away.

"But gradually, over the years, things have shifted. I was
so self-conscious about my situation that I stopped seeing most
people and, I guess by default, began to turn to my wife for
companionship. We started to travel. It was ironic . . . when
I had the money to travel first-class, we hardly went anywhere at all. But with the flexible schedule of academia I had
the opportunity to travel, and I found that I was able to enjoy
seeing new places even if my transport and accommodations
weren't top of the line.

"And my attitude began to change in other areas as well.
When I started to go downhill financially, we moved from our
big house to a small condo. At first I was humiliated by the
change, but then, when we did begin to travel, we discovered
how great it was to just pick up and leave at a minute's notice,
without making elaborate arrangements about looking after our
fancy house with all our expensive stuff while we were gone.

"So," he concluded, measuring his words very carefully,
"what has been a major regret, that clearly destructive decision to leave a successful job, now, near the end of my work
life and at nearly the end of my life itself, is no longer a regret
at all. In fact, I'm thankful, because I got out of that high-
pressured situation while I was still relatively young. After all,
in midlife I discovered my wife again. We have what I consider a remarkable closeness for a couple married so long, and
I know for certain that would never have been achieved in my
old life.

"Work is still not great, but the good part is that retirement, which I always feared when I was successful, I now can
hardly wait for. Providing we have our health, it should be in
many ways the best time yet."

As Marvin suggests, the prospect of and adjustment to
retirement differ widely. For some of us, the first morning we
wake up with no place to be at nine o'clock is the first day we

really feel old. Although our jobs are often a source of frustration and continuing stress, to lose work is to lose some considerable measure of identity. Already feeling life's physical
diminishment, we sometimes find the loss of meaningful activity adding greatly to the anxiety and regrets of aging.

Writer Wallace Stegner muses on what can be a harsh and
frightening reality after the retirement party is over. "The
companionship of fellow workers and the satisfaction of a
shared function turn out to be more valuable than we ever
thought while we had them. As the retired executive may yearn
for the sense of power and usefulness that his desk once gave
him, the ex-postman's feet wistfully remember the comfortable turnings and re-turnings of his old route. In short, more
people than would probably admit it find in work the scaffold-
ing that holds up the adult life."

What does happen when this structure no longer supports us? It's estimated that about one third of retired people
experience the end of work as a crisis. Many people become
disenchanted, disappointed, and even seriously depressed. This
seems especially true if we berate ourselves for having made
an investment in work that left little time to develop other
interests or relationships. When he reached the age of seventy-
six, psychologist Albert Ellis, the founder of the school of Rational Emotive Therapy, shared his fervent conviction that older
people need to find "a vital, absorbing interest," an activity,
cause, or hobby that is meaningful, dominant, and ongoing.
He encouraged older people to face later life with excitement
rather than despair. Just as it is more of a triumph to create a
fine meal or furnish an attractive home on a limited budget,
we should "enjoy the challenge of living with restrictions."

In terms of dealing with the physical and emotional losses
of aging that are beyond our control, the message Ellis offers
is really quite powerful. He is telling us that what we can control, and what we should take responsibility for controlling, is
our own response to such loss. Instead of wallowing in self-
pity over what we no longer are, or lamenting over what we
can no longer do, we should turn our interests enthusiasti-

cally elsewhere, where we can use both our remaining and newly acquired skills. "There are so many possible diversions that you can find," he says, "that your turning up with nothing absorbing is almost beyond comprehension."

Try again. Fail again. Fail better.

A final look at Georgia O'Keeffe's life reveals that when her vision began to fail in old age, and she could no longer paint, she took up pottery under the tutelage of Juan Hamilton. Sixty years her junior, he helped her find new sources of enjoyment in tactile sensation, in the feel and texture of clay. Putting aside her canvas, she seized the opportunity to continue creating in a new and vital way.

The lack of sexual expression can be experienced as another physical and also emotional loss in old age. Sex in our society is almost totally portrayed as the province of young people (except for the older man who is revitalized by the younger woman). Even in less youth-obsessed times, we linked greater age with diminished physical passion. As Hamlet says to his mother: "You cannot call it love, for at your age / The hey-day in the blood is tame, it's humble, / And waits upon the judgment."

Circumspect judgment does not—nor should it always—prevail over sexual yearning in later life. A sexually repressed man till late in life, Henry James met a young sculptor who apparently awakened dormant sensory feelings and a desire for physical love. In a letter to Hugh Walpole, James expressed his sense of waste over having waited so long to acknowledge these needs. (He also illustrates how we regret more what we didn't do than almost anything we actually did.) "I think I don't regret a single 'excess' of my . . . youth, I only regret in my chilled age certain occasions and possibilities I didn't embrace."

James's biographer Leon Edel believes that this new sexual and romantic awareness not only enhanced Henry James's last years but also enriched his final writing. "James had come to see at last that art could not be art . . . without love. He had become his own Sphinx, he was answering his own riddles."

Of course, in a youth-obsessed culture, it takes courage for an older person to admit sexual desire. "I suppose I'm not the typical older woman of sixty-four," Helen, attractive and very animated, told us. "I love being with younger men. . . . The ones my age are either married or too old and tired—no life, no spark. If I were a man, no one would think twice about the fact that I'm drawn to younger women. But being an older woman means you shouldn't have sexual feelings, or at least that you shouldn't admit them freely or, worst of all, act them out!"

Helen's initial burst of feeling subsided, and her voice calmed. "It's not that I hop into bed any chance I get with a younger man," she earnestly explained. "Most of the time I just enjoy flirting and kidding, and they seem to get a kick out of it. I have a great time with some of the younger guys at work. I enjoy going out for a drink with them at the end of a day, but yes, there are times I wish their company would extend through the night.

"I regret that I was so dominated by restrictive religious views on sex as a young woman, that I was really sexually repressed. It wasn't just that I held back from sex, but that I couldn't even enjoy it when it was sanctioned.

"I married right out of high school, and my husband was really a very boring lover. We couldn't talk about our sex life the way couples do today, let alone get professional help the way they do now. I used to daydream and fantasize about having affairs, but I never did, even though there were opportunities, because I was positive I'd be damned forever if I broke such an important commandment.

"Well, now, I'm not so rigid about what I think is sinful. And I feel that if memories of sex are all I'm going to have in old age, I wish I had tried to do something earlier on to see that they were more exciting."

Simone de Beauvoir summed up her own feelings about

the sexual losses of older women when she wrote, "A woman of seventy is no longer regarded by anyone as an erotic object. It would be most exceptional for an old woman to have both the means and the opportunity of getting herself a partner; and then again, shame and fear of what people might say would generally prevent her from doing so."

Still, more and more men and women are remaining sexually active well into old age. Many elderly people are fully capable of finding new ways of stimulating old passions. Theologian Paul Tillich, for example, made a convincing argument for the use of pornography in old age. If we can find excitement in an ordinary life, he said, by reading adventure novels, or distract ourselves from sorrow with amusing films or plays, why not find stimulation in erotica at a time of life that suffers from a lack of eroticism?

More important, perhaps, than whether or not sexual activity continues, we can celebrate old age's capacity for rich affectionate relationships. The years may bring the loss of treasured old friends, but with age's ability to understand the deep sustenance of friendship, we can savor each moment with those who remain, those Albert Camus referred to in a related context as "companions to our fate."

As we grow wistful over the inevitable disparity between the life we lived and the life we imagined we would live, we can acknowledge that our memories, good and bad, make up much of the atmosphere of this future we have finally arrived at. There is actually great relief in relinquishing our early illusions about a perfect, regret-free life that will, in fantasy, never end. Instead, we can accept, as Theodore Isaac Rubin puts it, that "I am a person, a person doesn't live forever, and can't accomplish and experience all things."

If we experience old age as a time of reconciliation with past regrets, leaving them behind as scenery that no longer supports our life script, we can let the play wind down and take our curtain calls with pride and peace.

THE CHALLENGE
OF REGRET

What difference does it make how much you have?
What you do not have amounts to much more.

—Seneca

Nine

Wealth, Fame, Power . . .
and Regret

"If I'm such a legend, then why am I so lonely?" asked Judy Garland. "If I'm such a legend, then why do I sit at home for hours staring at the damned telephone, hoping it's out of order, even calling the operator asking her if she's *sure* it's not out of order."

Often, we think that people with power, money, and fame are beyond the reach of regret over empty relationships, faulty choices, and unfulfilled needs. Yet, not only do the regrets of eminent men and women frequently mirror our own, their emotional pain can be particularly acute. For, along with the discrepancy between what is and what might have been is the contradiction between how the envious public views their lives and how unhappy they truly feel.

"Nobody believes me when I say I'm discontented with my life," one legendary businessman told us. "And certainly nobody's sympathetic. They think I'm impossibly greedy, that I only want more, or that nothing can ever satisfy me. They almost seem angry at me for not enjoying what I guess they think would make their own lives trouble-free."

As this man has discovered, "making it" guarantees neither self-confidence nor self-esteem; nor does it validate the choices made to reach such rarefied heights. Even when we are adept at denial, most of us sense that we have made some highly regrettable compromises along the way, and we feel painful stirrings of conscience. If we have allowed ourselves to measure success by someone else's standards, we can also experience discomforting feelings of self-betrayal.

The actor Montgomery Clift, serious about his craft, described his response to sudden film stardom. "There is the problem, which is not to do with acting. It is being that word— a star! You become public property." As public property, he was making choices that had more to do with maintaining the public's interest than with developing his talents, which led to this note of warning to a friend who also seemed on the brink of success: "If you have a goal—and you're busy growing—you're safe. It's only when you believe of yourself what the general public believes that you start losing the courage to risk outward failure. That is the biggest pitfall. *Look out!*"

Montgomery Clift seemed to understand that the failures that follow risk-taking in the pursuit of growth are regretted far less than the failures that come from playing it safe. "Failure and its accompanying misery is for the artist his most vital source of creative energy," he said.

If our goals are not genuinely self-defined, are superficial and aimed more to win approval than to develop mastery, failure can be a bitter, energy-draining blow. When the public began to lose interest in Montgomery Clift, he had already come to need their acclaim, and the loss made him increasingly depressed and self-destructive.

"It is through being wounded that . . . power grows and can, in the end, become tremendous," wrote Friedrich Nietzsche. As painful as failure can be to the public figure, it can become a powerful force for change. When Mario Cuomo lost the Democratic mayoral nomination in New York City in 1977, he had ample reason to regret his bid for the office, which had generally been considered ill-advised. His failure was humiliating and fed political gossip about his lapses in judgment because of stubborn conceit. Yet, according to biographer Robert McElwaine, the loss was a positive force in Cuomo's life. It brought him "a streak of humility that had not been especially evident before. Much of his apparent arrogance evaporated. He learned important lessons in defeat that probably would have remained unlearned had he won."

Some of these lessons were quite specific, explains McElwaine. Cuomo completely changed his speaking style, "abandoning the aggressive courtroom manner that he now realized was out of place in political oratory and debate." Although he has so far chosen not to run for the office, Mario Cuomo's political horizons today reach toward the presidency, not in the least because of his oratorical skills.

There are some basic differences between the stories of Mario Cuomo and Montgomery Clift, besides their response to a loss of popularity. As opposed to Clift's swift ascent, Cuomo's career, like those of many men and women in government, moved up the political ranks at a relatively even pace. One step led to another; one decision was based on another decision—good or bad—that had come before.

As we've touched on earlier, for many people in the arts—and today, in the business world as well—regret is nurtured by success that comes too abruptly, that brings too many lavish rewards before one is developmentally ready to handle them or to see the connections between choice and consequence.

During the 1980s, Wall Street was rife with youthful millionaires, and even billionaires, who found ingenious, and in some cases illegal, ways to quickly make phenomenal fortunes. It was estimated that Michael Milken, for example, who was fined $650 million for his financial misdeeds, had several hundred millions more left after the fine was paid.

Nonetheless, before pleading guilty, Milken felt the need to express his regret over his belated realization that greed's stain can spread to the lives of innocent bystanders. Through unchecked tears, he told the court, "I am truly sorry. . . . This long period has been extremely painful for my family and friends as well as myself. I realize that by my acts I have hurt those who are closest to me."

Although writing a best-selling book or play doesn't bring in the financial rewards of the stock market, there are significant hazards for a writer who makes a sudden leap from obscurity to celebrity, sometimes almost literally overnight.

Truman Capote's first novel was published to enormous fanfare when he was twenty-four. Although he was a celebrated writer and sought-after companion for many years, in a variety of ways his life steadily spun downhill. He would later reflect on the problems of his writing and social life. "I've asked myself a thousand times: why did this happen to me? What did I do wrong? And I think the reason is that I was famous too young. I pushed too hard too soon."

F. Scott Fitzgerald became a best-selling writer at the age of twenty-four. His and his wife Zelda's high-living antics seemed to embody the flamboyant values of the twenties. As the joys and rewards of fame faded, Fitzgerald wistfully recalled life before he had to confront its failed promise: "That first wild wind of success and the delicious mist it brings with it . . . a short and precious time—for when the mist rises . . . one finds that the very best is over."

As he examined the disparity between what success had brought and what he had once imagined it would offer, Fitzgerald commented that a "succeeding period of desolation and the necessity of going on" often follows early fame. Taking stock of the creative standstill at which he found himself, he saw that "I could no longer fulfill the obligations that life had set for me or that I had set for myself."

As Fitzgerald drank more and more, his gifts as a writer began steadily to diminish. He always deeply regretted writing a substantial part of *Tender Is the Night* while intoxicated, certain that it would have been a much better book had he been sober. As he sank deeper into destructive self-indulgence, Fitzgerald often felt a need to confess his regret to his editor and mentor, Maxwell Perkins. "It is only in the last four months that I've realized how much I've—well, almost deteriorated in the three years since I finished *Beautiful and Damned*," he wrote in one letter. "[I've produced] an average of about *one hundred words a day*. If I'd spent this time reading or traveling or doing anything—even staying healthy—it'd be different, but I spent it uselessly, neither in study nor in contemplation but only in drinking and raising hell generally."

"It is a mark of many famous people that they cannot part with their brightest hour," observed playwright Lillian Hellman.

Fitzgerald, with the sensitivity that marked much of his writing, was able to anticipate this wistful struggle in his own life, even before it actually took place. "I remember," he wrote to Perkins, "riding in a taxi one afternoon between very tall buildings under a mauve and rosy sky: I began to bawl because I had everything I wanted and knew I would never be so happy again." And indeed, years later, as his literary reputation waned he longed to be "extravagantly admired again."

Partly to pay for Zelda's care in a sanitarium, Fitzgerald went to Hollywood to work as a scriptwriter. He found the vocation demoralizing, despite considerable financial success, and always deeply regretted his break with books and fiction. Writer Budd Schulberg, a friend during the Hollywood years, saw Fitzgerald as part of an "American tragedy, a serious artist who aspired to the largest possible audience, a writer who needed a constant stream of gold." In what could be an epitaph for regret, Fitzgerald in Hollywood, concluded Schulberg, was a man who seemed to "live constantly in the past."

Now more than ever, we live in a culture that pits self-indulgence against the desire to build a meaningful life, which gives Fitzgerald's story particular value. Zelda's does as well, for she was a woman who could not give up her youthful fantasies of extravagant achievement.

When she was nearing middle age, Zelda Fitzgerald, who still clung to her youthful though erratically pursued dream of becoming a prima ballerina, went to Italy to dance and study. Nearing exhaustion from frantic efforts to perfect her skills in a small ballet company, she was finally told that, although she was talented and could hold her own with the dancers, she would never become a prima ballerina.

Even though her accomplishment was impressive—she had managed to earn herself a place in a professional group at an age when most dancers have passed their peak—she was so crushed that she left dance altogether. She was unable or unwilling to modify her youthful dream in ways that could bring her midlife pleasure, remaining instead, to the end of her increasingly unhappy existence, a captive of unconstructive regret.

Dylan Thomas, whose first book was published when he was only twenty years old, embarked on perhaps the most epic course of self-destruction in literary history. While still a young man, Thomas believed his talents were already used up. His friend, the writer and critic John Malcolm Brinnin, explained: "I knew as well as he that his unhappiness lay in the conviction that his creative powers were failing, that his great work was finished. . . . Now that he had arrived, he was without the creative sources to expand his position. As a consequence, he saw his success as fraudulent, and himself as an impostor."

Feeling like an impostor is a ubiquitous experience in our own times. Psychologist Lawrence Shames reports on research into the "impostor phenomenon," which shows that as many as 40 percent of highly successful young men and women privately "know" they are "faking it." No matter what heights they achieve, and how confident they seem about their accomplishments, they feel like "bluffers, vulnerable at any moment to exposure and disgrace. . . . So fragile was their self-esteem . . . that the smallest thing—a question they couldn't answer, a small gaffe at a meeting—could send them plummeting into anxiety and depression."

Clearly, having to act like supermen and women, exerting enormous decision-making power when developmentally we are not fully mature or broadly experienced can lessen the rewards of even the most powerful corporate post or creative achievement, by making us feel we truly don't deserve or won't be able to sustain what we've won.

Athletics is a field in which youth and accomplishment are, by contrast, a more natural fit. We expect accomplished athletes to be young, and we don't ask them to be anything but physically adept. Nevertheless, it is often difficult to build a rewarding adult life in the wake of early fame.

A popular fictional character is the basketball or football hero, such as the protagonist in Irwin Shaw's story "The Eighty-Mile Run," who desperately clings to the role that brought him premature success. He stays far too long at the game, until he is sometimes humiliatingly dismissed from the arena because his skills have clearly failed him. When he finally does move on, memory continues to dominate current experience, and reality pales in comparison to what his life once was.

Those who manage to retire from sports with grace and a minimum of regret have understood, while the cheering still rang in their ears, that it was a sound that wouldn't last forever.

Kareem Abdul-Jabbar was interviewed on the first day of his retirement from basketball. In an empty stadium, leaning back in a seat usually occupied by a roaring fan, he gazed down on the scene of his triumph. Despite the scenario's potential for regret, the reporter found the basketball hero "serene."

Kareem, at forty-two, was closing out a basketball career that spanned twenty years with the NBA, a record unmatched by any other player in the history of professional basketball.

It is a record that brings a comfortable feeling of closure to boyhood dreams. "No regrets," he said firmly. "I've had a wonderful career . . . it couldn't have been better. I can recall growing up in New York and hoping that some day I might be able to play one pro season with all those great players. I outlasted everyone." Kareem found enormous satisfaction in remembering the dreams of his boyhood, and knowing that he had fulfilled them beyond even his most fantastic aspirations.

Kareem Abdul-Jabbar was able to use the accomplishments of the past as a source of pleasure and pride, rather than as a measure of what will be missing from his life in the future. Too often, particularly in the rapacious atmosphere of modern life, our achievements serve only to feed new, more grandiose goals, which prevents us from finding satisfaction in personal accomplishment and relationships.

Living in the past is a potential problem for anyone who, like the aging athlete, achieved self-esteem and celebrity primarily through qualities that are clearly transient. For many women, particularly in a culture like our own which equates youth with beauty, growing older can cause a terribly painful separation from happier times.

Ava Gardner, who was always admired more for her face and body than for her acting ability, claimed that she could appraise her life as an aging woman with hard-eyed clarity. "Honey, there comes a time when you're an old broad. . . . I've had a hell of a good time, so my face looks, well, lived in." She added, in a mocking, defiant tone, "You won't find me standing in front of a mirror, weeping."

Ava Gardner once was the object of the volcanic passion of some of the world's most famous men, from Howard Hughes to Frank Sinatra: "No one ever loved a woman the way Frank loved Ava Gardner," said Sinatra's biographer Kitty Kelley. Trying to let go of that glittering past, Gardner refused to furnish her London apartment with mementos of those liaisons.

"I don't like all that stuff hanging around. . . . I don't need to be reminded every minute."

Sophia Loren is a woman of more stable impulses than Ava Gardner, and she has also built a more substantive career as a serious actress. "Aging is very relative," she said, concerning her regrets over growing older. "I try to keep myself in shape as much as I can, but getting older is wonderful. You mature. You experience so many things. Joy. Sorrow sometimes. But I've had a wonderful life."

While there are some things she would change if she had the chance to correct past choices, Miss Loren staunchly maintains that, at this point in her life, "I have no regrets." Her reason is clear: "I'm proud of what I've done with myself."

And indeed, Sophia Loren is an example of someone who uses the painful lessons of the past to define her goals and energize her efforts to reach them. The illegitimate child of a man who abandoned her, Sophia Loren grew up in poverty and hurtful anonymity. "I always felt I had no father," she said in a *Parade* magazine profile, although she said she never complained about her deprivation. "Even when you're young, you get accustomed to the negative things in life. You say to yourself, 'Maybe it has to be like this.' "

The fact that she was able to accept this unfortunate beginning kept her from being mired in bitterness over the past, and allowed her to concentrate on the future: "I knew I wanted to do something in life. I didn't want to be anonymous." To fulfill this promise to herself meant struggling against all kinds of obstacles, including aspects of her own personality. "I have always been very shy," she confesses. "When I first meet somebody, I don't feel at ease. It's always very difficult for me. Journalists always ask me how I can be so calm and sure of myself in front of the camera. They don't know what I have to go through to appear like that."

Continuing her reflections, Ms. Loren said that when she visits her mother (who figures greatly in her daughter's success) they spend hours talking "about what's happening and what's going to happen," glorying in the realization of those long-ago dreams. "My God," they say to each other. "It still works. The dream never ends."

Obviously, Miss Loren's pleasure in what she has been able to achieve counteracts many of her regrets over growing older. Looking at her life on a continuum, she sees her future as vital and filled with possibilities. "If I really put my energies into something, it happens." After all, she explained, "I never thought . . . that I was going to be as successful as I am. Now everything sounds very easy, like I've done everything with a magic stick. But there were lots of sacrifices and risks."

Similarly, when he was well past seventy, the actor Burt Lancaster challenged an interviewer: "Why don't you ask me about taking risks? That's where you'll find the real Burt Lancaster. I determined long ago—and they thought I was crazy—not to keep doing roles I was so popular in."

As he grew older, Lancaster continued to grow more impressive as an actor. As he suggested, he could have played it safe by continuing to do parts that the public admired and identified him with and to make films that would be sure commercial successes. Instead, as the *New York Times* film critic Vincent Canby noted, "For each mass-market entertainment film he made, there was always one comparatively risky 'artistic' venture."

Lancaster's determination to "be an actor," rather than a "hero," was strengthened by his regret over agreeing to change the ending to the movie *Apache*. The studio felt that the public would object to their hero, played by Burt Lancaster, being killed.

"For a while, I wouldn't reshoot the scene, but I finally gave in. I never forgave myself for doing that. This was a good movie, and that ending would have made it a classic. After that, I said, 'Never again.' My life is not just my career. It's more important."

Carol Burnett agrees that risking failure adds to rather than prevents overall growth, and diminishes the regret of self-betrayal. She also illustrates how, if we have a basically strong

sense of self and feel good about an accomplishment, the criticisms of others hold less power over us. "Lots of projects that
I've done have flopped. What I've learned, though, is that if I
like my own performance, I'm not nearly as bothered as I am
when I don't like what I've done. That's when I want to kick
myself. If I like what I've done—even if no one else likes it—
I can handle that failure much easier."

In her personal life Ms. Burnett took the very great risk
of ending a twenty-year marriage. "It's disorienting," she admitted. "There have been times . . . when I've felt I was
treading in quicksand." However, when asked if she regretted
her decision to divorce, she answered, "No, I don't. Even with
the loneliness, the self-doubt, the uncertainty . . . these feelings still exist in me . . . but . . . I have a tomorrow."

Like Sophia Loren, Carol Burnett believes that whatever
tomorrow brings, she will be ready for it. Having also survived many earlier pains, from an unhappy childhood in an
alcoholic family to a failed marriage, "you know you can survive. And that is a good thing to know."

Clearly, the self grows stronger, and we regret past experiences less, as we survive struggle and loss. We may not
fail if we never risk trying to succeed, but we will also not
develop into people to whom we can offer our own respect.

Not long ago, the death of a seventy-nine-year-old woman
named Marie-Madeleine Fourcade was announced. She had
been a leading figure in the French Resistance during World
War II, and the only woman to lead a major network of Resistance fighters against the Nazis in France. Miss Fourcade was
captured, and then escaped, but her life was shadowed by
danger and the constant threat of death. Yet, interviewed on
television shortly before she died, she said, "Deep down, I
ask myself if those years were not the best of my life. Certainly, there was fear. When one was hunted, the fear strained
you permanently, stopping you from sleeping and living. But
it became part of the character, and I do not regret this character."

Few of us will ever face the kinds of choices that Miss

Fourcade made, but all of our lives are marked with singular moments of courage, when we choose not to regret the loss of personal integrity that often follows giving in to our fears.

"My father was a very powerful man," remembered the actor Kirk Douglas. "He was a man who drank a lot as a form of escape, and I have often thought that one of the bravest moments in my life was when I was about ten, and we were all sitting around the table drinking tea. I took a spoonful of tea and flicked it in his face. Well, he grabbed me, spanked me, but I just felt satisfied to have done it, and it was almost like an act that saved me."

In her own memoir, Lauren Bacall, looking back on her life, greatly regretted not exhibiting this sort of defiant strength when her principles were trampled. "I don't like or admire myself for not having the courage to stand up to Howard Hughes every time he made a crack about Jews," she said, adding that it took many years to forgive herself for her inability to risk her employer's wrath by challenging his bigotry.

The regret over acts of omission or commission to people we care about weighs heavily on most people, even when they are lauded by a public of strangers. Ernest Hemingway mourned that his life was "often very distasteful due to the mistakes that I have made, and the casualties to various human beings involved in that sad affair."

Eras of political and social unrest often breed casualties to innocent people, and regret to those who may have contributed to their pain. Noted television producer Mark Goodson recalled the "dark terror" of the television blacklisting days of the 1950s, when alleged communist sympathizers were kept from writing, directing, or appearing on TV. Goodson looked back, and unhappily decided that while he did his best to stand up to the blacklist, he didn't take an aggressive enough stance against the hysteria it engendered. "I can't help the feeling," he reflected in an article for *The New York Times*, "that if I'd shown more courage, if I'd stood up earlier, if more of us had been willing to take the heat, we could have brought that disgraceful era to a more rapid close."

Playwright Arthur Miller was similarly troubled by the House Committee on Un-American Activities hearings in the 1950s and their effect on the theater and films. Congressional investigators attempted to bully him and other witnesses into naming "communist sympathizers in the arts," in order to save their own careers. Miller remembered that he was driving back to New York after a visit to Salem, when he heard on the radio that his friend Elia Kazan had given in to the pressure and provided a list of their colleagues to his interrogators.

"Numbness held me," Miller recalled. Knowing how deeply Kazan valued the people whose names he had revealed, Arthur Miller went on to write the play *The Crucible*, which in its story of the Salem witch hunt depicted how "the destruction of meaning seemed total when the sundering of friendships was so often with people whom the witness had not ceased to love."

The anguish of feeling responsible for some beloved person's pain becomes almost unbearable when we know we will never have a chance to try again to heal it. Poet Robert Frost grieved over his failure to communicate to his young adult son some message that could have penetrated the isolating despair that eventually resulted in the boy's suicide. "I took the wrong way with him," Frost lamented. "I tried many ways, and every single one of them was wrong. Something in me is still aching for the chance to try once more. That's where the greatest pain is located."

Sometimes, it is not what a prominent person did or did not say that caused someone else pain, but simply that they chose to follow a particular, personally necessary course. Writer Edna O'Brien's first novel, *The Country Girls*, was, to her surprise, a great success; and to her even greater surprise, its success heralded the end of her marriage.

"I think men are frightened of certain professions, particularly of writers," she said on reflection. "And I would say that I have had to pay, to pay that price in my life, and it wasn't that I wakened up one morning and said I choose my career rather than a happy, loving, lovely domestic life. I actually want both, but it doesn't seem possible."

The writer Neil Sheehan was more fortunate in his determination to follow compelling creative goals. His book about Vietnam, *A Bright, Shining Lie*, took sixteen years to write, getting him and his family $300,000 in debt before its eventual and by no means certain successful publication. Unlike Miss O'Brien's husband, however, Sheehan's partner in marriage always fully supported his dream, and happily shared in his eventual triumph.

Clearly, there were many things Sheehan did not do because of the limits the project placed on his life, and he knows now, sixteen years later, that he may never do some of these things at all.

"Some days I wake up and I think, 'I'm not young anymore. I've got a bum knee. . . . But then I think, what the hell, age catches up with you whatever you do, and I've been lucky." Because he was home writing while his children were young, "I saw more of our daughters than most fathers do, and I wrote the book I wanted to write." His wife agreed. "One pays a price for whatever one does," she said. Her own contribution to the book's creation surely helped her cope with her regrets over their huge investment of money and time.

With a similar ability to place personal values over other people's ideas about what constitutes a significant life, the writer, actor, and entertainer Noel Coward assured admirers that "It must not be imagined that I was not beset by doubts. . . . In my deep Christian subconscious, there was a gnawing suspicion that I was nothing but a jester, a foolish, capering lightweight with neither depths nor real human understanding. That, immediately after my death, if not a long while before, my name would be obliterated from public memory. For long years I searched to find a theme solemn enough on which to base a really important play."

And then, he recalled, one day it suddenly "came upon me in a blinding flash, that I had already written several important plays—important because they had given a vast number of people a great deal of pleasure."

Noel Coward might have been more appreciated as a serious critic of social behavior if he had chosen to write in a different, more somber genre. But allowing himself to appreciate the writer he had become finally diminished the regret stirred by fear that other people would see his contributions as insignificant.

Simone de Beauvoir, a woman the world took very seriously indeed, was nonetheless intermittently haunted by the questions that always accompany regret: How might I have lived a different life? Would it have been a more meaningful one than the one I have chosen? "I do not know where I might have been led by the paths that, as I look back, I think I might have taken, but that in fact, I did not take," she mused. She reconciled herself to the basically unanswerable question by deciding that overall her choices in life had seemed necessary and valid, and had brought her to a point where she was "satisfied with [my] fate."

When we see ourselves as pawns, never really choosing at all but wandering aimlessly on random paths without realizing how they are connected to our future, then we can arrive at the future filled with regret over lost opportunity and an absence of meaning. Tennessee Williams, when asked by a biographer whether he had any regrets, replied quickly, and with passion, "Oh, God, yes, baby. So many things to regret, . . . I don't feel any continuity in my life. It is as if my life were segments that are separate and do not connect."

Happily for his audiences, Tennessee Williams was able to use his pain and bewilderment as powerful creative material. His writing reflects a lifetime of courageous self-assessment, and acceptance of the deepest kind of regret. Williams's characters reveal themselves to one another and to themselves through language that resonates with despair and disappointment over their often bitter mistakes—language that Williams himself categorizes as "cries of the embattled heart."

Writer Graham Greene noted that "writing is a form of

therapy; sometimes I wonder how all those who do not write, compose or paint can manage to escape the madness, the melancholia, the panic fear which is inherent in the human situation."

Other people whose pasts are filled with mistakes but who continue the struggle to turn their lives around can find great poignancy in success. Actor Charles Dutton was singled out for his brilliant performance in the Pulitzer Prize-winning play *The Piano Lesson*. Although Mr. Dutton is a graduate of the Yale Drama School and has the manner of a man whose major challenge in life was grooming his career, he has a history of violence and imprisonment.

Raised in a ghetto where crime was endemic and even celebrated, he stabbed and killed someone he claimed had attacked him and began a prison career at seventeen that did not end until he was twenty-six years old. While in prison, Mr. Dutton was stabbed in the neck by another inmate, an occurrence that finally illuminated the price he was paying for the life he had chosen to follow. Then, instead of continuing to try to prove that he was as tough and fearsome as his fellow convicts, he decided to separate himself from their experience and values. "I told myself that I had followed these guys into hell, and right now, I was in hell with them."

In an amazing story of determination and ability, Dutton went on to college and graduate school, after doing preliminary academic study, and even acting, while still in jail. As critical acclaim poured in after the premiere of *The Piano Lesson*, he said, "My years in prison are . . . often in my mind. Ten years of my life were wasted away. Sometimes I forget about it, but then it comes back. Like opening night . . . at that tremendous curtain call.

"I was standing there, bowing with the rest of the cast, listening to all the applause, and suddenly, I thought, 'Fourteen years ago, it was a bunch of inmates who were applauding me.' "

It was a remarkable, bittersweet moment. Smiling and bowing at the cheering crowd, he knew that those lost years would never be reclaimed, but he could also take grateful pride in thinking, "God . . . I've come a long way."

Where we have arrived, and how long it has taken us to get there, are the sum of all our choices and mistakes. Neither fame nor wealth seems to lessen this fundamental truth. Indeed, Tennessee Williams ultimately concluded that wealth and fame often were not life-affirming but, instead, could destroy the ability to grow. The security of success is often a catastrophe, he said. It can become "a kind of death . . . no less terrible than dying poor and unknown in a dingy room," simply because it takes place "in a storm of royalty checks beside a kidney-shaped pool in Beverly Hills."

Williams offers us a final reminder that whatever we have managed or failed to achieve, we need to persist in the struggle to move beyond regret. "It is never altogether too late," he says, implying that while we may have missed opportunity in the past, we must pay attention now so that we can recognize and seize it when it passes by again:

"Ask anyone who has life. Live. Time is short, and it doesn't return. . . . It is slipping away while I write this, and while you read it, and the monosyllable of the clock is, Loss, loss, loss, unless you devote your heart to its opposition."

To strive, to seek, to find, and not to yield.

—ALFRED LORD TENNYSON

TEN

Coping with Regret

When Alexander the Great met the philosopher Diogenes, he asked the legendary teacher if there was anything he could do for him. Diogenes had a simple request: "Only stand out of my light." In this final chapter, to supplement the suggestions we have offered elsewhere in our book, we present you with additional material on how to use regret constructively. We hope to provide you with knowledge that will illuminate the path toward self-understanding, and the tools with which to cope more successfully with life's inevitable mistakes and failed dreams.

Self-awareness and skills to free us from regret's restraints cannot develop overnight. We're aware that this might be considered heresy in an age that expects immediate solutions to all problems, but we assume it has already become clear to readers that always wanting to feel better *now* often deepens distress—self-blame sets in when impossible hoped-for changes don't occur right away.

In contrast to an earlier chapter, where we discussed the less-effective psychological defenses that breed unconstructive regret, we will now examine the more effective defenses that are valuable weapons against emotional pain. We will also describe other psychological techniques that can be used as well, to keep regret from creating emotional anguish.

179

Effective defenses shield us from more stress than we can handle, and encourage ways of thinking, feeling, and behaving that allow us to adapt more successfully to the stressful situation. They allow us much more flexibility and are a more mature response to threat. Perhaps most important, these positive defenses can operate at the conscious level, so that we can deliberately use them to manage the tension both of current choice and of past decisions we deeply regret.

The first effective defense at our disposal is *altruism*, feeling genuinely good because we have done something positive for others. Contrary to the narcissistic messages of contemporary culture, compassion and doing for others positively shape our sense of self and our sense of purpose in life. Living in a culture that sanctions greed and selfishness doesn't encourage us to develop defenses like altruism, but they are vital and necessary tools in dealing with life's array of commitments and choices.

Altruism helps us deal with stress all through life, and indeed, it contributes to the sense that no matter what our age, we are still actively engaged in living. On her seventy-fifth birthday Eleanor Roosevelt said, "When you cease to make a contribution, you begin to die. Therefore, I think it a necessity to be doing something which you feel is helpful in order to grow old gracefully and carefully."

In reflecting back in his old age, Albert Schweitzer regretted his meager personal life, especially the fact that he hadn't devoted himself more to his wife and child. On balance, however, he was serene, for he "had blessings too: that I am allowed to work in the service of mercy."

Too often today, individual need and fiercely protected autonomy have taken precedence over the powerful source of happiness that can be found in empathy and a desire to help. Even women, who have traditionally been nurturers and found meaning in their nurturing, have been affected by our culture's devaluation of altruism. As the eminent psychologist Jean Baker Miller explains, "Although women in general have a much greater sense of the importance of a feeling of connection to other people, this sense of connection . . . has not been given its full value in the dominant culture. Instead, it has been disparaged, and this . . . has led to women disparaging themselves for feeling its importance."

Yet, for the most part, even though they are rightly demanding more independent lives, women, who generally come to generativity earlier than men, continue to understand how caring for others enriches the life experience. As proven by such groups as the Big Brothers and the Hospice movement, which helps people cope with terminal illness, the ability to reach out is crucial to men's lives as well.

In a small New England town, Vince, a middle-aged shopkeeper, "adopted" a cancer patient about his own age through Hospice. "With all the people in the world, I felt that no one should be alone or die alone," Vince said, to explain his involvement. Once a week, sitting at the dying man's kitchen table, the two men drink tea and talk over subjects ranging from the most mundane to the patient's fear of death. Vince feels he has benefited immeasurably from the relationship. He says firmly, "I've received a lot."

Developing a sense of altruism helps us understand that as social beings, we can't review every past decision or approach every new one simply from the perspective of self-gratification. It will help us understand that any choice we make has to be looked at through a lens colored by commitment toward others. *Measuring our regrets over missed opportunities against how our decisions benefited others can soothe self-blame and increase self-compassion.*

"If I am not for myself, who will be? If I am only for myself, what am I?" asks the Talmud. Roberta recently celebrated her twenty-fifth wedding anniversary. At the celebration her husband offered a loving toast that moved Roberta to tears. As the evening progressed she reflected on how ten years ago she had ended a brief but passionate love affair when the man pressed her to leave her husband and start a new life.

"I loved my husband, but we married young and had children early, and to my mind we had settled into a prematurely predictable life. I guess, despite my love for my family, there was a yearning for a kind of excitement I had only experienced very briefly when I was much younger.

"I had never known anyone like Kevin. We met by accident, but it was an overpowering response, and despite my misgivings and fears, to my amazement I found myself in an affair. He and I shared an incredible number of interests, and he was utterly brilliant. Besides the overwhelming physical attraction, I could talk to him for hours. Believe me, only something as powerful as this could have overcome my guilt over what I was doing. I simply couldn't give him up."

Nonetheless, when pressed to end her marriage, Roberta sent her lover away. For a long time thereafter she obsessed over how wonderful life might have been if she had decided differently, and she tormented herself for not being courageous enough to break free of convention.

"But gradually," she said, "I realized my choice was based on much more than convention—on my responsibilities and sense of commitment. Nothing, no matter how exciting, could compensate for my being the cause of any suffering to my children, or to my husband, who is such a genuinely good and loving man."

By focusing on the love and gratitude she felt for her family, Roberta was able to find comfort for her loss. "I've come to feel that not only would their unhappiness have diminished my contentment, because of my guilt, but on a positive scale, I have a real sense of well-being now, without feeling at all like a martyr. My husband is truly pleased with our life, and in many important ways, like having a real sense of commitment, I am too. My kids are building stable lives of their own, and I measure all this against my regret about what I gave up, or think I gave up. It makes the regret a great deal easier to live with."

Besides the positive power of selfless behavior, *altruism can also be a way to ease painful regret over once having been too self-centered.* When Ellen moved to Chicago from a small town in upstate New York, her younger sister, Annie, begged to go with her and finish high school there. Ellen knew that their alcoholic father was creating an ever more chaotic home environment, and that without Ellen there to lend support, her sister's life would be considerably more stressful. "But I really wanted to be free to come and go in a way that having a teenager living with me wouldn't allow. So I talked her, and myself, into the idea that it would be better if she stayed and finished school where she had started. I told her she could come to me after graduation if she still wanted to.

"A few months after I left, my father came home drunker than usual one night, and started beating up my mother, which was the first time there had been any physical abuse, and when Annie tried to come to her defense, he started hitting her. She left that night and went to her boyfriend's house. His parents put up with the situation for a few days, but when they told Annie that she couldn't stay there permanently, both of the kids took off. They didn't call me, which pains me terribly, because it shows how deeply alienated Annie felt from me. They did not come back to finish school, and now seem to be wandering around the West Coast taking odd jobs. They keep in touch with my mother and with his parents, but have never given any permanent address. Of course she never writes to me," Ellen finishes with a sigh.

It's been nearly three years since Ellen saw her sister, and she despairs over the idea that the relationship will never be renewed. She worries deeply about her sister's future, and is plagued with regret over abandoning Annie at a time when— she now acknowledges—the younger girl's need for protection and guidance was clearly greater than her own need for privacy and freedom. "There's no way I can delude myself that my choice wasn't totally selfish."

While Ellen can't completely eliminate her guilt over her sister, she has dealt with her regret in two very constructive ways. Instead of prolonging the resentment she always felt toward her mother for being so passive, she has actively worked to help her mother change her life. Through Ellen's encouragement, her mother has joined Al-Anon, which helps nondrinking members of alcoholic families. And while she remains with her husband, Ellen's mother is finding new strength and courage through the group's support. As a more direct attempt to make up for not having helped Annie, Ellen is actively involved in working with troubled girls through the Big Sisters service organization.

"I realize I'm trying to compensate for what I didn't give to my real sister," she says. "And obviously I know that these efforts won't help Annie, but I feel a lot better knowing I can help someone else before they reach Annie's predicament. I've learned how important it is for kids to feel they have someone they can count on to care about them, and I feel very rewarded by helping them cope with circumstances that seem too much to handle on their own."

Coping Strategy

Examine your regrets. Concentrate on and assess how people you care for benefited by the selfless course you took rather than the course you think would have provided your own personal gain.

If you regret having hurt someone through selfishness in the past, try to find ways to demonstrate altruism in your current life. Even if altruism doesn't come naturally to you, do something unselfish that will benefit other people. Whether this involves simply listening better to someone who needs understanding, or volunteering for some service role, try to strengthen undeveloped altruistic aspects of your personality. The more you behave like an unselfish person, the more spontaneous and integrated this kind of behavior will become.

The next positive defense is *suppression*. This is not to be confused with repression, in which we automatically push a painful feeling or problem completely out of awareness. Using suppression, we make a conscious and purposeful decision to temporarily defer confronting a problem that seems overwhelming. Psychiatrist George Vaillant explains that the defense of suppression involves "deliberate postponing but not avoiding. One says, 'I will think about it tomorrow.'" Unlike repression, the major proviso, Dr. Valliant reminds us, is that *"the next day one remembers to think about it."*

Brad and Joan, like many other couples, have had the continuing struggle of trying to find the right time and place to deal with problems that come up in their marriage. The common scenario is that they find themselves in bed at night, both of them exhausted and feeling increasingly detached from each other because the underlying issues that separate them have still not been dealt with. Joan can't fall asleep because of her frustration over this inability to resolve their problems, and she tries to start a discussion. Brad sighs with irritation and reminds her that he has an important meeting in the morning and can't stay up half the night arguing. His resistance adds to her frustration, and she becomes openly hostile, which he returns in good measure. The end result is that both become so agitated that a real battle ensues and one of them flees the bedroom to sleep on the living room couch.

While Joan insisted that she needed to talk to Brad when she did, because they never seemed to have any other opportunity, the time she chose was not at all conducive to her goals. She would have been better off telling him that she was very upset, and although she didn't want to initiate a late-night argument, she did need a commitment from him about when they could talk during the next day. This way of using suppression—temporarily postponing dealing with the source of her frustration—could be in itself a step toward better resolution. Even before the talk takes place, Brad's pledge to her for a specific time to discuss their problems would defuse the tension that keeps her awake and increasingly angry with him that night.

A temporary delay in dealing with emotionally laden issues can be adaptive and healthy, and it avoids the pitfall of a hasty, panic-driven outburst or, as often happens, taking an impulsive action that almost always exacerbates our problems. Suppression is a deliberate decision to buy some time for further thought, or to wait for a more opportune moment to seek some solution.

Suppression can also help us adapt to circumstances that are beyond our control. We commonly do this with such anxiety-producing occurrences as trips to the dentist, when we tell ourselves that although we dread going, we'll ultimately feel better for having gone. Our fear and discomfort is held at bay when we concentrate on the situation's positive aspects.

Similarly, we can suppress our obsessive focus on past mistakes that we cannot correct and, instead, deliberately look for the positive features of our actions and decisions. In this way, we can consciously use suppression to seek out the possible benefits of a negative experience.

Coping Strategy

If anxiety over dealing with a problem is causing you great stress and you're not realistically able to handle it immediately, set aside a specific time in the very near future with the person or persons involved to begin the process of resolution. If you are alone and must plan independent strategies, try writing down the steps you will soon take to deal with the concern.

When you begin thinking about past regrets, try to unearth any positive aspects to the experience, including what you've learned from your unwelcome action and/or decision. Suppressing the negative will help to free you from its crippling constraints.

*   *   *

Another of our effective defenses is a sense of *humor*.

By exaggerating or diminishing a situation, humor helps us cope. It offers another, lighter version of a difficult reality.

Some of life's most painful experiences can be eased by our ability to laugh at ourselves. Paradoxically, humor is often a barometer of human suffering. Nietzsche summed it up precisely: "The most acutely suffering animal on earth invented laughter." In times of famine, people make jokes about food; in oppressed societies there are jokes about free speech. There are death-camp jokes and poverty jokes, and no ethnic joke is told more often and with greater humor than by the ethnic person himself.

Woody Allen invariably infuses his films with jokes about love and death, clearly using the screen to work through his most obsessive personal concerns. ("What is it about death that bothers me so much?" he asks—"Probably the hours.") Many counselors feel that a sense of humor plays a crucial role in a client's potential for recovery. The ability to laugh at ourselves, to see the absurdity of a situation, can lighten even unbearable pain.

Eugene has always regretted his social ineptness. He can't seem to make small talk; he's a clumsy dancer. A man in his late thirties, Gene is eager to be married, but time after time relationships fizzle out. Recently he had a brutally humiliating experience at the beach house in which he had forced himself to rent a share. The camaraderie of a group of strangers was potentially very threatening, but he was determined to give the hoped-for "new Eugene" a try.

Almost immediately, he became greatly attracted to one of the other renters, and to his delight, although they never went out alone together, she seemed equally interested in him. "I told everyone in the city that I had met someone special, and on the third weekend that we were going to be together, I decided I was really going to go for it. I bought myself a whole new set of beach clothes. Then, when I got off the ferry, I bought flowers and champagne, and made a reservation for dinner at the island's best restaurant—of course without asking her. Can you believe such idiocy?

"I was thrilled when I got to the house and found that no one else was there but her. I took a deep breath and handed her the flowers, put the champagne down on the table, and pulled her toward me, aching to finally kiss her. All of a sudden, over her shoulder, I see her bedroom door open and this naked guy comes out carrying a towel. We all stood there frozen, just staring at each other, and then she says, 'Gene, I'm so sorry . . . I thought you knew. This is my fiancé.'

"I can't even attempt to describe what I felt like. I wanted to cry, and in fact, tears did begin to well up. I just turned around and walked out of the house and down to the dock and took the next ferry back to the mainland. My heart was pounding in my ears all the way back to the city. I kept attacking myself for being such a fool, for being so needy that I'd built up this fantasy of what could be. . . . I didn't know how I was ever going to face anyone, let alone her, again.

"But one night soon afterward I just felt I had to talk to somebody about it because I felt so terrible, and I went to see a good friend. I started to describe the scene, and he was trying to be sympathetic, but when I got to the part where her boyfriend came out naked, my friend suddenly burst out laughing. At first I was furious, and he started to apologize but he just couldn't stop laughing, and all of a sudden I found myself laughing too.

"We both got caught up in playing variations with the scenario . . . speeding up its action and accentuating the 'drama'—like one of those old Charlie Chaplin movies or French farces. You know: me clapping my hand across my forehead in dismay . . . the lover desperately trying to cover his crotch, 'our' girlfriend clutching her heart and gasping in horror. The exaggeration really dissipated my shame. I laughed, admittedly somewhat hysterically, but it suddenly didn't seem nearly as momentous. I acted like a fool . . . but who doesn't have something like that in their closet?"

It may not seem possible to consciously call on the defense of humor. After all, aren't some people simply not funny? In truth—although certain people do have a much more highly developed wit and comic perspective—most of us have the capacity to find at least some comedy in a potentially ludicrous but painful situation.

Humor is a particularly useful defense against regret, because a primary cause of regret is the failure to measure up to idealized standards of perfection. Perfectionists can't allow any leeway for mistakes or shortcomings, and feel only anger and humiliation when they fail to reach their impossible goals. Humor challenges these harsh judgments and helps us to accept our less-than-perfect selves in a less-than-perfect world.

Coping Strategy

If you regret behaving in an embarrassing way, don't let the embarrassment block out the situation's comical aspects. Think about how amusing the situation might seem if you weren't the central player.

Ask yourself if you are blocking yourself from using humor as a defense because of some resistance to the response, such as the idea that it's immature to laugh things off.

Understand that humor is a vital part of the human experience, and that you can use it to enrich your life.

Anticipation is especially helpful in preventing future regret. It involves thinking ahead to difficult situations and trying to come up with a strategy to cope with what we may encounter. While we often worry about things that will never materialize, what distinguishes anticipation is that it is useful for situations we can reasonably assume *will* occur.

Crystal's daughter, Mary, is in her last year of high school. While they experience a normal amount of mother/daughter conflict, their relationship is quite strong. It has grown particularly so during the last few years, when Crystal has been raising Mary as a single parent. Recently, Crystal has found herself falling into periods of melancholy as Mary excitedly prepares to enter college several hundred miles away. Crystal is happy that her daughter will be going to the college of her choice, but she already feels bereft and tries to lessen her sadness by not dwelling on the idea of Mary's leaving.

"I'll cross that bridge when I come to it," she said, brusquely dismissing questions about how she feels about Mary's upcoming departure. It would be more helpful to Crystal to cross that bridge now. Anticipating what life will be like with her daughter gone could help Crystal avoid a very troublesome regret after she leaves: that she didn't handle this major transition in their lives well.

If she were to think ahead specifically about what changes there will be in her life and in her relationship with her daughter, she could plan more carefully for these eventualities. She could, for example, introduce some new interests into her life to make up for the approaching "empty nest." Most important, perhaps, she could plan ways to make the best use of the time she and Mary still have together, so that after Mary leaves, Crystal won't regret having wasted this precious period of conclusion to their more cloistered relationship.

Anticipating the loss of someone old or seriously ill will not make the death easier to take, but will make coping with the inevitable problems easier when death occurs. We may, for instance, seek counseling before the death takes place, or begin to straighten out financial matters that will seem overwhelming when we're actively grieving. We may also want to make the very best use of the time we still have together, not putting off visits or expressions of love, or even settling old issues so that they don't continue to plague us after it is too late to bring them to closure.

Anticipatory regret differs from the defense of anticipation, but as we saw in an earlier chapter, it is also an important tool in avoiding unconstructive regret. Employing anticipatory regret when facing a decision will enhance the quality of our choices, for they will be based on a careful inventory of pros and cons rather than an attempt to bury underlying anxieties and doubts under impulsive actions.

The process of how we make a decision has much to do with our ability to handle its consequences. Knowing that we have seriously considered various alternatives, their risks, and their potential for regret increases our ability to accept our choices even if they turn out poorly.

Coping Strategy

When you know that an event or change is going to occur in your life, begin thinking ahead to what you need to do to prepare for it, now and later on. Do your best to see that you acquire the tools to handle the new situation.

When you are considering an important decision, remember that even an apparently good and uncomplicated decision may have hidden pitfalls or consequences.

Gather information and talk to people like yourself who faced similar choices, and learn what their regrets were after the choices were made.

Seek out people whose perspective is different from your own to acquire a more objective view of the situation.

After weighing all the evidence, decide whether you are willing and feel able to handle the potential consequences of your choice.

All these defenses help move us toward the final common denominator in coping with regret: compassion for our personal limitations, and realistic appraisal of the reasons for our mistakes.

There are additional coping strategies at our disposal. While healthy defenses deal primarily with responses to stress on a *feeling* level, these other strategies deal mainly with how we *think* about a stressful situation.

To cope with regret, we can also *reframe* a situation so that we see it from a different, less obsessively focused perspective. Often the way we think about an experience, rather than the experience itself, determines how well we handle it. Attitude is crucially important in how we adapt to change in our lives. As we noted earlier, while our decisions can't be altered, our attitudes can.

Alexis is a pleasant-looking woman in her middle thirties. Although she has never considered herself attractive, she has a good job and feels confident about her ability and intelligence and, despite a relative absence of men in her life, was basically contented. Recently, however, she became quite depressed over the breakup of a seven-month-old relationship that she had believed was going to culminate in marriage. Her intractable regret and self-blame for the rupture of these dreams immobilized her to the point that she could barely function.

It is not uncommon to be depressed about the end of a love affair, but what kept Alexis so crippled by despair was that she could not find any reason but her own inadequacy to blame for the breakup. In fact, the dissolution of the relationship might have been due to any number of factors: She hadn't really known the man very long, and so hadn't really had the time to discover his true character, values, or goals. Maybe he had even deliberately misled her, or—and this is only human—maybe she wanted so much to believe it would work out that she overlooked or chose to minimize some visible flaws.

With some help from a therapist, Alexis overcame her self-blame by examining some of these other possibilities. In effect she was able to hold the situation up to a different light, *reframe* it so that her vision focused on another line of sight.

Instead of "He didn't want me because I wasn't good enough," she tried to think instead, "What I had to give he didn't appreciate." Also, when Alexis first met her lover, her mother had just died and her father had turned to his daughter to ease his pain. Allowing herself to feel compassion for her many burdens, Alexis now changed another thought. Instead of saying "I should have known better than to let myself fall for such a shallow man," she said instead, "Maybe I would have chosen a better partner if I hadn't been so understandably hungry for emotional relief."

Most important, Alexis was able to stop believing "I will never get over this loss" once she began to think "I am suffering this much because I feel deeply about people I love, and that's a hard but a good thing. What's more, I can learn from this pain to be more careful about what kind of person I allow to come into my life."

Reframing may look as if we are simply placing a different label on the same experience, but we are really doing much more than that when we change our view of an experience. As philosopher José Ortega y Gasset explains, "In each thing [there is] a certain latent potentiality to be many other things." Reframing can offer relief from our relentless examination of a particular regret by showing us our "mistakes" from a different perspective. In this way, reframing can help us be less destructively self-critical, for when we think we are at fault for a problem, we automatically forget any other mental perspective but self-blame.

Another strategy that deals with how we think is the technique of *"thought stopping."* This is particularly helpful in dealing with obsessive thoughts about what we "should" have said or done. These guilty thoughts, so often attached to regret, make us feel excessively culpable for usually exaggerated mistakes and imagined offenses.

If we find ourselves obsessively replaying a past experience, the first step is to recognize that we are needlessly tormenting ourselves, and that we are capable of stopping this behavior.

Rather than trying to resist the intrusive thoughts, we can remind ourselves that they are temporary and will pass. This will help us relax in their initial presence and say, "They're here, but they're not worthy of my attention and aren't important enough to waste energy on." Then, with sharp emphasis, we deliberately turn our attention to something else in order to replace the disturbing idea with another thought.

This deceptively simple technique allows us to transfer our energy from resistance to effective coping with intrusive thoughts. It is rather like the host who tells unexpected guests that he cannot entertain them and then goes about his business, instead of trying to pretend that he didn't hear them at his door, and sneaking around the house to avoid detection. Although by temperament and personality some people are always prone to obsess over their behavior and mistakes, employing such strategies can make guilty thoughts surface less often and not linger as long when they do.

Another tool for coping with regret is to *surrender the need to be right*. Too often, without consciously understanding what we're doing, we confuse surrender with weakness, even though, as Theodore Isaac Rubin points out, "Pride in nonsurrender of ideas and fixed positions renders us stubborn, rigid, constricted and impervious to learning and to growth. . . . For most of us, the inability to surrender can be destructive in our daily lives."

Alfred described a long cold war with his sister, the specific genesis of which had almost been forgotten. "We both have reason to be angry over a number of issues, and I just wasn't going to be the one to take all the blame and apologize when she was as wrong as I was."

However, now nearing fifty, Alfred found himself wanting to get past the cool civility of his relationship with his only remaining sibling. Early in our interviews he told us: "I intensely regret having missed sharing so many important occasions, happy or tragic, like our children's graduations, or my wife's recent illness, with the one person besides my wife and children who is family."

When we suggested to Alfred that this kind of regret did

nothing but immobilize him from trying to improve his relationship with his sister, he first protested that he didn't believe that anything he did could heal so long a rift. "Yet, I do know," he added thoughtfully, "that any level of friendship would be better than this anonymity . . . especially when I find myself obsessing about how close we once were. I guess you're right. Losing some pride by making the first overture seems worth the gamble."

Soon afterward, Alfred called his sister and tried to arrange a meeting. Although he was genuinely conciliatory, she tersely rejected his offer to meet and talk. Yet, rather than feel humiliated by her rejection, Alfred is grateful that he was able to swallow his pride and try to make amends. Although he still regrets his lost relationship with his only sister, he knows that he will blame himself less for its demise.

An effective psychological technique, which Alfred employed to lessen the pain of his sister's rejection, was to write a letter to her in which he freely vented his anger and hurt. "I knew I would probably never send it to her," he said with a slightly sheepish smile, "but it helped me get a lot of things I felt off my chest." It was indeed better for Alfred to write the letter and then put it aside (to read from time to time when he starts feeling troubled) than it would have been to attack his sister when they spoke. That kind of direct assault would probably have left him with more guilt, and certainly would make an already painful ending that much uglier and harder to resolve in himself.

Another coping strategy involves strengthening our capacity to *seize the moment*. Millie is a warm, unusually open woman in her mid-forties. It was clearly very important to her to tell us her poignant story. "Twenty years ago I was in the hospital for what the doctors thought might be a very rare contagious disease. Until the diagnosis was clear, only my mother and husband were allowed to visit me. My zany brother Allen, whom I adored, drove all the way down from Canada to see me and somehow had gotten a doctor's coat to wear. Late one afternoon while I was lying there feeling scared and sorry for myself, in he came dressed in that white coat and carrying a doctor's bag, which turned out to be a toy. For a minute I thought he really was another doctor, and when I realized it was Allen, I just burst out laughing. I was actually both thrilled and terrified at the same time.

"He started talking and joking, but I couldn't relax because I was so worried that someone was going to come in and he would get into trouble. I'm the big sister and I always worried about that crazy streak in him, even though it made him so lovable. Within a few minutes, just what I was afraid of happened. A nurse came in and started to get really angry, but then—I couldn't believe it—he actually managed to charm her into not only letting him go without reporting him, but giving us a couple more minutes to say goodbye. But you see," Millie said, her voice growing softer, "I was still so uptight that I couldn't enjoy the time with him, and was even relieved when he kissed me goodbye. He made one more comical face before closing the door behind him.

"I know this sounds unreal, but on his way back to Canada he was killed in a car accident. When I heard the news all I could think of was that I couldn't let myself enjoy him for those few wonderful minutes. From that moment on, I resolved never to let outside pressures get to me so that I disregard my real feelings and let an important moment go by. Sometimes I forget what I've learned, but when I do, I take out my wallet. When Allen visited me, inside that silly doctor's bag was a bottle of candy pills. He had given it to me when he was horsing around. To this day I carry that little bottle in the change compartment of my wallet. All I have to do when I forget is look at it, and I remember instantly the lesson I learned in such a hard way so long ago: to make the most of and live every minute you're graced with."

Millie's understanding of the importance of seizing the moment has altered her perspective and behavior in life. She feels she has become a more open and spontaneous person, and is far more willing to take risks in pursuit of personal happiness. Those of us who don't have Millie's dramatic reason for changing our values and behavior often find *that deciding to live in the present is a bridge to a more satisfying future, and lessens the pain of self-blame over past mistakes.*

Without denying our regret, we can remind ourselves that while the moment we mourn is gone, we can seize and make better use of the moments that remain. This attitude will also make us better risk-takers, because, since our major aim will be to live more fully, our behavior will be less restrained by a fear of change.

After many satisfying years of teaching at a large city college, Leslie was appointed dean of the school of arts and sciences. He did not like handling all the administrative detail, but was determined to make a success of the prestigious job. For a few years Leslie kept on with the work, which was really more of a chore than a source of stimulation and pleasure, and eventually a new president was brought into the college.

"I knew I should have resigned at the time, as many other deans were doing so that he could bring in his own people. But I just hung in for a variety of reasons, even though it was clear he and I were very different kinds of people, as well as different kinds of administrators. Our relationship grew more and more combative, and I knew in my heart that I should get out before things got worse and go back to teaching, which I genuinely missed. But still, out of a mixture of stubbornness and inertia, and a concern about what I would do if I did leave—I didn't think I'd want to go on teaching there, and jobs at my level weren't so easy to come by anywhere else—I stayed on.

"Anyway, shortly after the first year of his administration, he let me go in a very public and extremely humiliating fashion. I was devastated, not just at the horror of the firing, but at my absurd refusal to see the handwriting on the wall that had created this mess in my life."

Leslie resigned from teaching and suffered a period of serious depression. "But with help, I began to work on making my life as good as I could by figuring out what I could do *now* to make my life enriched. I very consciously took advantage of opportunities that I might once have let pass by, and created others for myself. For example, I volunteered to work as a guide in a major museum, and when they discovered my teaching background, they offered to pay me for giving lectures to visiting students. I take people on walking tours of the city and other art museums, and I love every bit of all the work.

"I also began to travel much more, and I've bought a share in a summer colony for artists and writers, so that for several months a year now I'm in the company of people that give me the sense of community I used to feel at the college. I still regret not leaving the deanship while there was time to reconstruct my academic life there, but by this concentrated effort to live *now*, I'm gradually feeling less obsessed by my really serious mistakes in the past."

All these defenses and strategies are genuinely important and useful, but *no matter how willing we are to fight the battle against regret, there are times when even regrets we think have been resolved can surface, and sometimes with unexpected force.*

For instance, the birthday of someone no longer in our lives, perhaps through death or divorce, stimulates regret over issues never resolved and failures of love. Our own birthdays can prompt us to rethink choices and mull over goals not yet realized. In the wake of nostalgia, a high school or college reunion can carry competitive regret with our classmates that is far more troublesome than the comparative shape of our bodies. As we measure our personal and professional achievements against theirs, the years seem littered with the debris of our own foolish choices.

Holidays often have a bittersweet tinge as, moved by sentimental songs and traditional rituals, we remember our own ghosts of Christmases past. And then, with the approach of a new year, we can feel like the Roman god Janus with his two faces, who was able to look backward and forward at the same moment. As midnight chimes a year's passing and another's beginning, we assess the old year's unresolved regrets, and wonder if this new one will allow us to surmount them.

We all experience some of this cyclical regret. In fact, on any given day, for any number of reasons, we might feel more or less troubled by its haunting presence. Overall, however, if we are dealing with regret constructively, we are usually able to believe that the feeling will pass. As one man put it on a beautiful day in Cape Cod: "When I look out at that ocean, I don't have many regrets—or at least I can cope with them. On a bad day back in the city when my boss chews me out, they can seem a good deal worse, and I'm much harder on myself for the mistakes that created them."

While regret *is* transitory, we are often not conscious that some of our own thinking and behavior will contribute to and even breed more regret. We should observe ourselves for these characteristics which usually appear in polarized extremes. Once we acknowledge the presence of these traits, we can work on modifying them before the regret they contribute to becomes too entrenched:

• Habitually procrastinating or avoiding important decisions, or rushing headlong into impulsive action.
• Relying too much on other people's opinions, or resenting advice even from people we respect.
• Anguishing over unimportant details and unknown risks in potential choices, or refusing to reflect on possible consequences.
• Experiencing continuous self-doubt and blame, or never reflecting on any of our decisions.
• Raging at ourselves over setbacks, or denying any anger while showing clear signs of hostility toward others or to ourselves.

Being sensitive to these kinds of behavior will certainly help us greatly in avoiding new regret, which can plague future life. However, there may well be periods when coping with old regret seems beyond our corrective abilities or skill, and it is helpful to have some guidelines to decide whether professional help may be called for.

If even minor losses or setbacks continue to cause great pain; if we are unable to learn from our mistakes and continue to repeat them; if we can't bring ourselves to make amends that are still possible; if we can't make some compromise or find a suitable alternative to a stressful situation; when our roles as parents, partners, students, or workers are affected by our regrets; or when obsessive looking backward brings feelings of depression, then some professional counseling will likely be helpful.

Still, since regret is a normal feeling, most of us, most of the time, can find ways to deal with it on our own. For some people, this may simply mean being unusually generous to ourselves. "When I feel myself slipping back into 'if-only's' I indulge myself with something," said a woman who had made several major errors in her early life. "I go to the movies, or buy a special treat at the market, or exercise to make myself feel good about my body. Or, even though I'm normally tight with a dollar, I do something that really gives me enormous pleasure, like calling my oldest friend, who lives across the country, and staying on the phone with her for a really long talk—the hell with the expense."

Using such tactics as limited self-indulgence can certainly help us through a bad, regret-laden day, but putting regret into what we have called a livable context requires more complex solutions, such as our healthy defense systems and related strategies. While we can't erase irreversible decisions, make bad choices into good ones, or erase all the pain over what might have been, we can initiate corrective action— whether that takes the form of developing compassion for ourselves, making amends with other people, trying to find positive lessons in our mistakes, accepting compromise choices, or forging a new perspective on an unmistakably regrettable situation.

What is crucial to remember, no matter what path we take to healing, is that whatever our age or wherever our wrong or missed turns have brought us, there is still time to turn our regrets into a constructive life force. For, while yesterday does remain the irreversible past, as Kafka wrote, "The decisive moment is perpetual."

Appendix: Inventory Scoring and Self-Empowerment Worksheet

Regret: Your Own Story

In choosing to read this book, you have already taken a major step toward understanding regret's remarkable influence on all of our lives. You may still not be clear, however, about regret's specific place in your life. How much of your experience is shadowed by a yearning for what might have been? This book is an attempt to enhance your knowledge about, and acceptance of, this important and natural human feeling. Awareness is always the first step toward any important change in our behavior or attitudes.

The inventory you took at the beginning of the book and the Self-Empowerment Worksheet that follows are tools that will heighten your awareness through self-evaluation. As we noted earlier, since regret is often masked by or connected to other feelings, we do not always recognize its presence or the degree of its intensity. These materials will help guide your journey toward constructive ways of coping with regret.

Remember that no examined life is completely free of regret, but you *can* try to see where your life falls on regret's continuum. When you complete this evaluation you should be in a better position to decide what steps you need to take to turn regret into a force for constructive change.

The suggestions for change that we have presented in our book, however, will be only as useful to you as you are honest about making a self-appraisal. The aim of the inventory and worksheet is to empower *you* to take more control of your experience, for we believe that with enough self-awareness, people are not only able to diminish their regret but can find the power to change their lives.

Inventory Scoring

Using the following directions, go back to the inventory on pages 3–5 and figure your regret level.

Scoring

Add up your total score. For every question unanswered because it doesn't apply to your life (such as one pertaining to parenthood if you have no children), add 1 to your total score. Find your regret level in the table below:

Total Score

121–140	A high level of regret; requires working at some coping skills.
81–120	An overall moderate level of regret; may require some working on specific troublesome issues.
51–80	A low level of regret; either coping effectively or tending toward some denial.
50 and below	A likelihood that denial is covering awareness of regret.

Self-Empowerment Worksheet for Regret

Answer these questions as thoughtfully as you can, using all the ideas and principles introduced in the book and the self-inventory, referring as often as needed to specific pages. This exercise does not lead to a score, but to personal insights that can serve as a guide for important changes in your relationship to regret. Think of this as a combination of a personal journal and a practical blueprint.

1. If you could change something (pick one issue at a time) you've done in your life, but now wish you hadn't done, what would it be, and why?

   a. How strongly do you feel now about this issue? Has your response lessened at all over time?

   b. How much do you blame yourself for what happened?

   Do you think the amount of self-blame is realistic?

   If "yes," can you now modify the behavior (impulsivity, selfishness, etc.) that created the past problem?

   c. Is there anything you could do now to lessen your regret about this situation? For example: making amends to someone, trying to feel more self-acceptance and compassion, seizing an important moment now, forming new interests.

2. Is there something you haven't done in your life, but now wish you had?

   a. How strongly do you regret this omission now?

   b. How much do you blame yourself for it? Is this degree of blame realistic?

    c.   Is there anything you can do to redress this omission now (taking more current risks, making corrections in other areas of life where it is still possible, reaching out more, reframing)?

3.   If you could change something that happened in your life but that you had *no control over*, what would that be?

    a.   Do you continue to blame yourself for something that was beyond your control?

    b.   What can you do about this now?

4.   How much of a gap, if any, do you feel in your life between "what is" and "what might have been"?

5.   Which of the *healthy defenses* and other coping strategies discussed in this book can help you cope better with your regrets at this point in your life?

6.   Which *ineffective defense* might you be using that you need to be more aware of?

7.   Using all of the material presented in the book, and your own ideas as well, what would your self-change program look like right now?

Be specific. For example, select major regrets and list which particular healthy defense(s) or coping strategy would work best to alleviate its stress.

    Break your plan into steps. When will you begin and what will you do first? Begin with the most manageable action and move toward more difficult steps. For example, if you regret a rift in a relationship, you might first work on surrendering the need to be right; next, try to reframe the situation so that you see it from a different perspective; and then go on, step by step, until you feel you want to and are ready to take the risk of reaching out to the person you would like to be close to again.

Work slowly and steadily.

Don't expect results overnight.

Remember that change occurs in small steps, but changes do accumulate over time so that you can become a person *who feels better about the past and lives more fully in the present.*

Chapter Notes

Introduction

Robert Sugden, "Recrimination and Rationality," *Theory and Decision*, Vol. 19 (1985).

Chapter 1

Galway Kinnell, "Prayer," *The Past* (New York: Houghton Mifflin, 1985).
Karen Horney, *New Ways in Psychoanalysis* (New York: W. W. Norton, 1939).
Daniel J. Boorstin, *The Image: Or, What Happened to the American Dream* (New York: Atheneum, 1962).

Chapter 2

Karen Horney, *Neurosis and Human Growth* (New York: W. W. Norton, 1950).
Martha Nussbaum, *The Fragility of Goodness* (Boston: Cambridge University Press, 1986).
"Conversations with Martha Nussbaum," Bill Moyers, Public Broadcasting Co., 1988.
Henry Geldzahler, *American Painting in the Twentieth Century* (New York: Metropolitan Museum of Art, 1965).
R. D. Laing, *The Politics of Experience* (New York: Ballantine Books, 1967).

Chapter 3

John Cheever, *The Journals of John Cheever* (New York: Knopf, 1991).
Jane Smiley, *New Woman*, July 1988.
Erich Fromm, *The Anatomy of Human Destructiveness* (New York: Holt, Rinehart & Winston, 1973).
Erich Fromm, *To Have or to Be* (New York: Harper & Row, 1976).
Abraham Maslow, *Toward a Psychology of Being* (Princeton, N.J.: Van Nostrand, 1962).

Hans Selye, *The Stress of Life* (New York: McGraw-Hill, 1956).

Lawrence Cherry, "On the Real Benefits of Eustress," *Psychology Today,* March 1978.

May Sarton, "Now I Become Myself," *Selected Poems of May Sarton* (New York: W. W. Norton, 1978).

Chapter 4

Rainer, Maria Rilke, *Letters to a Young Poet* (New York: Random House, 1984).

Reuven Bar Levan, *Thinking in the Shadow of Feelings* (New York: Simon & Schuster, 1988).

Karen Horney, *Neurosis and Human Growth* (New York: W. W. Norton, 1950).

Karen Horney, *Self-Analysis* (New York: W. W. Norton, 1942).

Betty Friedan, *The Feminine Mystique* (New York: W. W. Norton, 1963).

Richard Gotti, "Love and Neurotic Claims," *The American Journal of Psychoanalysis,* Vol. 42, No. 1 (1952).

Leon Festinger, *A Theory of Cognitive Dissonance* (Evanston, Ill.: Row, Peterson, 1957).

William Walster and Elaine Walster, "Choice Between Negative Alternatives: Dissonance Reduction or Regret?" *Psychological Reports,* Vol. 26 (1970).

Jack Brehm and Robert Wicklund, "Regret and Dissonance Reduction as a Function of Postdecision Salience of Dissonant Information," *Journal of Personality and Social Psychology,* Vol. 14 (1970).

Irving Janis and Leon Mann, *Decision Making: A Psychological Analysis of Conflict, Choice, and Commitment* (New York: Free Press, 1977).

Robert Sugden, "Recrimination and Rationality," *Theory and Decision,* Vol. 19 (1985).

Chapter 5

Clark Moustakis, *Psychotherapy with Children* (New York: Harper & Row, 1959).

Alfred Adler, *The Problem Child* (New York: Putnam, 1963).

Arthur Jersild, *Child Psychology* (Englewood Cliffs, N.J.: Prentice-Hall, 1968).

Anthony Storr, *Solitude* (New York: Free Press, 1988).

Alice Miller, *Prisoners of Childhood* (New York: Putnam, 1963).

Andrew Merton, *The New York Times Magazine,* September 2, 1990.

John Updike, *Self-Consciousness* (New York: Knopf, 1989).

Chapter 6

Joseph Campbell, *The Power of Myth* (New York: Doubleday, 1988).

F. Scott Fitzgerald, "Early Success," *The Crack-Up* (New York: New Directions, 1956).

"Women's Lives, A Scorecard of Change," *The New York Times,* August 20 and August 21, 1989.

"Proceeding with Caution," *Time*, July 16, 1990.

Daniel Levinson, *The Seasons of a Man's Life* (New York: Knopf, 1978).

"Women," *Time*, December 4, 1989.

Jean Baker Miller, "The Development of Women's Sense of Self," Paper presented at the American Academy of Psychoanalysis Conference on Women's Emerging Identity, October 1, 1983.

Carol Gilligan, *In a Different Voice* (Cambridge, Mass.: Harvard University Press, 1982).

Henri, Robert, *The Art Spirit* (Philadelphia: J. B. Lippincott, 1923).

Robert Nozick, *The Examined Life* (New York: Simon & Schuster, 1989).

Richard Kinnier and Arlene T. Mehtha, "Regrets and Priorities at Three Stages of Life," paper presented at American Psychological Association, Washington, D.C., August 1986.

Chapter 7

Mark Strand, "The Story of Our Lives," *Selected Poems* (New York: Atheneum, 1984).

Galway Kinnell, "Pont Neuf at Nightfall," *Mortal Acts, Mortal Words* (Boston: Houghton Mifflin, 1980).

Roger Gould, "Adult Life Stages, Growth Toward Self-Tolerance," *Psychology Today*, February 1975.

Roger Gould, *Transformations* (New York: Simon & Schuster, 1978).

David Karp, "For Many, Turmoil of Aging Erupts in the 50's," *The New York Times*, February 7, 1989.

Bernice Newgarten and Nancy Datan, "The Subjective Experience of Middle Age," *The Life Cycle* (New York: Columbia University Press, 1981).

Daniel J. Levinson, "The Midlife Transition: A Period in Adult Psychosocial Development," *The Life Cycle* (New York: Columbia University Press, 1981).

Theodore Isaac Rubin, *Compassion and Self-Hate* (New York: Macmillan, 1975).

Erik Erikson, *Gandhi's Truth* (New York: W. W. Norton, 1969).

Sophie Freud Lowenstein, "The Passion and Challenge of Teaching," *Harvard Educational Review*, Vol. 50, No. 1 (February 1980).

"The Simple Life," *Time*, April 8, 1991.

Chapter 8

Erik Erikson, Personal correspondence, July 28, 1988.

Erik Erikson, Joan M. Erikson, and Helen Q. Kivnick, *Vital Involvement in Old Age* (New York: W. W. Norton, 1986).

Erik Erikson, ed., *Adulthood* (New York: W. W. Norton, 1978).

Harvey Lehman, *Age and Achievement* (Princeton, N.J.: Princeton University Press, 1953).

Robert Butler, "The Life Review: An Interpretation of Reminiscence in the Aged," *The Life Cycle* (New York: Columbia University Press, 1981).

Saul Bellow, *Herzog* (New York: Viking, 1961).

Robert McNamara, Interview. *Time*, February 11, 1991.

Lee Atwater, *Life*, February 1991.

Anna Quindlen, "Regrets Only," *The New York Times*, February 7, 1991.

Michael Argyle, *The Psychology of Happiness* (London: Methuen, 1987).

Phillip L. Berman, *The Courage to Grow Old* (New York: Ballantine Books, 1989).

Simone de Beauvoir, "Joie de Vivre," *Harper's*, January, 1972.

Victor Frankl, *Man's Search for Meaning* (Boston: Beacon Press, 1963).

Robert Atchley, *Social Forces and Aging*, 6th ed. (Belmont, C.A.: Wadsworth, 1991).

Chapter 9

Katinka Matson, *Short Lives* (New York: William Morrow, 1980).

Robert McElwaine, *Mario Cuomo* (New York: Scribners, 1988).

F. Scott Fitzgerald, *The Crack-Up* (New York: New Directions, 1956).

Laurence Shames, *The Hunger for More* (New York: Times Books, 1989).

"Milken Pleads Guilty," *The New York Times*, April 25, 1990.

John Daniell, *Ava Gardner* (New York: St. Martin's, 1982).

Sophia Loren, *Parade*, January 18, 1987.

Burt Lancaster, *Parade*, November 6, 1988.

Carole Burnett, *New Woman*, February 1989.

Albany Times, Marie-Madeleine Fourcade obituary, July 21, 1989.

Kirk Douglas, *The Ragman's Son* (New York: Simon & Schuster, 1988).

Mark Goodson, "If I'd Stood Up Earlier," *The New York Times Magazine*, January 13, 1991.

Arthur Miller, *Timebends* (New York: Grove Press, 1987).

Neil Sheehan, *The New York Times*, April 15, 1990.

Natalie Bober, *A Restless Spirit* (New York: Atheneum, 1981).

Noel Coward, *Present Indicative* (New York: DaCapo Press, 1980).

Harry Rasky, *Tennessee Williams: A Portrait in Laughter and Lamentation* (New York: Dodd Mead, 1986).

Chapter 10

George Valliant, "Defense Mechanisms," *The New Harvard Guide to Psychiatry*, ed. Armand Nicholi, Jr. (Boston: Belknap Press of Harvard University Press, 1988).

Rollo May, *Freedom and Destiny* (New York: W. W. Norton, 1981).

Irving Janis and Leon Mann, *Decision Making: A Psychological Analysis of Conflict, Choice, and Commitment* (New York: Free Press, 1977).

Index

A

Abdul-Jabbar, Kareem, 167–168
Acceptance of regret, 128–129
Addiction, 18–19
Adler, Alfred, 79
Adolescence, regret in, 82–83
Adult consciousness, 112
"Age and Achievement" (Lehman), 140
Alexander the Great, 179
Alice in Wonderland (Carroll), 115
Allen, Woody, 19, 187
Altruism, 180–184
Ambition, regret and, 11–12
Anger, 8, 10
  about career, 122–123
  case of parent with handicapped child, 62–64
  in children, 88–90
  Chinese character for regret and, 22
  constructive expression of, 89
  converting to compassion, 32–39, 129
  outward focused, 22
  self-reproach (inward focused), 22–32, 111, 123

turning against the self and, 62
Anticipatory regret, 112–115, 189–191
Apache (film), 170
Arendt, Hannah, 129
Argyle, Michael, 151–152
Assertiveness
  lack of, and regret, 43–44, 89, 122
  positive, in achieving goals, 44, 124–125, 127
"At War with My Skin" (Updike), 90
Atwater, Lee, 144–145
Autonomy and independence, 13–16
  behavioral freedom, 17–18
  cases of regret and, 15–16, 17–18

B

Bacall, Lauren, 172
Baldwin, James, 21, 41
Bar-Levav, Reuven, 58
Beauvoir, Simone de, 157–158, 175
Beckett, Samuel, 152
Behaviors contributing to regret, 199–200
Bellow, Saul, 143
Birthdays and regret, 198–199

213

Bitterness, 23–26, 31, 128, 129
    case of giving child up for adoption, 41–43
Boorstin, Daniel J., 12
Brahms, Johannes, 139
Bright, Shining Lie, A (Sheehan), 174
Brinnin, John Malcolm, 166
Brown, Ron, 145
Brown University, 36
Burnett, Carol, 170–171
Butler, Robert, 142, 145
Byron, George Gordon, Lord, 118

C
Campbell, Joseph, 48, 94, 106–107, 129
Canby, Vincent, 170
Capote, Truman, 164
Career, regret and
    cases of, 20, 95–97, 98, 99–100, 103–104, 110–111, 197–198
    delayed choices and, 110–111
    early success, 97–100, 163–167
    enriching disappointing career, 124
    idealization of lost opportunities, 55–56
    lack of risk-taking and, 49
    middle age reassessment and, 121–125
    O'Keeffe, Georgia, 36–37, 104–105
    risk-taking in, 52–53
    women executives, 102–103
    women at midlife, 136–137
    See also Fame and regret.
Carner, Mosco, 139
Carroll, Lewis, 115
Cheever, John, 41
Chesterton, G. K., 137
Childlessness, regret and, 95–97, 126
Children and regret
    cases of control issues, 87, 88, 89–90, 91–93

cases of failure to seize an important moment, 81–85
cases of lack of risk-taking, 75, 78, 79–80
constructive choices, how to teach, 76, 78–79, 85–87
death and, 91–92
divorce and, 92–93
failure to seize an important moment, 81–87
fear of being laughed at, 77, 79
fear of rejection, 80–81
fear related to risk-taking, 77
gender distinctions and regret, 93–94
grandparents and positive effects, 150–151
issues of control, 87–93
Merton, Andrew, and child's independent choice, 86–87
resolving fears, 78, 79
self-blame in, 85
self-image in, 90–91
sharing feelings, 78, 79
solitude and, 81
survey of regret in, 76
Updike, John, and control issue, 90
values and, 87–88, 94
Choice
    behavioral freedom and, 17–18
    in childhood, 76, 78, 84–87
    constructive choices, how to teach, 76, 78–79, 85–87
    contemporary culture and, 10–13, 19–20, 37, 57, 84, 100–101
    decision-making technique, 112–115
    delayed and regret, 110–111
    exaggerated claims and, 69–70
    failure and, 13, 19
    illusion of having no, 43, 85
    loss and, 8, 10, 119

making a, 30
in middle age, 119, 125, 133
moral conflict in, 36
O'Keeffe, Georgia and, 36–37, 104–105
in old age, 155–156
personal values and, 20, 46, 47
precedents, lack of, 16–17
responsibility for, 76, 90, 191
self-deception and, 71–72
wrong, case of making a, 31–32
in young adulthood, 96–97, 100–102
Clift, Montgomery, 162, 163
Cognitive dissonance, 70–71
Compassion, 64
childhood resolution of fears and, 78
See also Altruism; Self-compassion.
Competitiveness, 11, 44
Conrad, Joseph, 141
Consumerism, 12, 19
Coping with regret
accepting responsibility, 56, 90
altruism, 180–184
anticipation, 112–115, 189–191
confronting illusions, 56
humor, 186–189
inappropriate self-blame, awareness of, 22
individual approaches, 200
reasons for choices, awareness of, 30, 132–133
reframing, 192–193
seize the moment, 195–197
self-compassion, developing, 32–39
suppression, 184–186
surrender the need to be right, 194–195
thought-stopping, 193–194
Country Girls, The (O'Brien), 173

Coward, Noel, 174–175
Cowley, Malcolm, 149
Creativity, 139–140
Crucible, The (Miller), 173
Culture, contemporary
adult responsibilities in, 97
assertiveness in, 43–44
choices in, 10–11, 12–13, 19–20, 37, 57
freedom in, 109
images vs. ideals in, 12
instant gratification in, 18–19, 179
marrige, values and, 108
mobility in, 16–17
personal gratification in, 13, 18, 165–166, 180
reexamination of values in '90s, 100–101
and regret, 10–20
self-centered entitlement in, 70
values of, 10–20, 43–44, 100, 129–130, 168–169
Cuomo, Mario, 162–163

D
Dante (Alighieri), 125
Datan, Nancy, 125–126, 127
Death
anticipatory regret and, 190
Atwater, Lee, 144–145
children and regret, 91–92
of loved one, and regret, 26–28
middle age and parental, 135
old age and, 140–141
Decision making
anticipatory-regret technique, 112–115, 189–191
procrastination and, 115
support system for, 115
Defenses against regret, positive, 179–180

Defenses against regret (*cont.*)
  altruism, 180–184
  anticipation, 189–191
  humor, 186–189
  suppression, 184–186
  See also Coping with regret.
Defenses, psychological, 179
  denial, 57, 58–61, 67
  exaggerated claims, 69–70
  false pride, 69
  intellectualization, 64–66
  rationalization, 66–67
  repression, 61–62
  turning against the self, 62–64
  unyielding regret, 68–69
"De-illusionment," 133
Denial, 57, 67, 128
  Holocaust and, 58
  ineffectiveness of, 58–59
  of past, example of, 59–61
Depression, 8
  case of, and regret, 29–30
  O'Keeffe, Georgia and, 37
Despair, 142
"Dialogue of Self and Soul, A" (Yeats), 39
Diogenes, 179
"Disguised parent," 107
Divorce
  Burnett, Carol and, 170–171
  career conflict and, 104
  children, regret and, 92–93
  delaying and regret, 126–127
  grandparents and support for children, 151
  statistics, 104
  vasectomy and, 113–114
Douglas, Kirk, 172
Dreams
  case of parent and denial of child's unhappiness, 61–62
  incest victims and, 61
  therapeutic value of, 62

Dukakis, Michael, 144
Dutton, Charles, 176–177

E
Edel, Leon, 156
Education
  cases of regret and, 121–125
  older students, 121
  regret connected to, 45–46, 83–85, 120–122
"Eighty Mile Run, The" (Shaw), 167
Einstein, Alfred, 81
Eliot, T. S., 115, 123
Ellis, Albert, 155–156
Emotions
  case of executive at midlife, 136
  childhood, 76, 78, 86, 88–89
  defenses, psychological and, 58, 191–192
  denial and, 57, 58–61, 67, 128
  female self-effacement and, 93–94
  intellectualization and, 65–66
  rationalization and, 66–67
  regret as, 8, 203
  repression of, 61–62, 86, 144
  suppression of, 184–186
Erikson, Erik, 108–109, 135, 139, 142, 149–150
Erikson, Joan, 149–150
Eustress, 53
Exaggerated claims, 69–70
Exley, Frederick, 13

F
Failure, 13, 19, 44
  growth from, 162–163
  Luce, Clare Booth and, 46
  in old age "fail better," 152
  success in, 106
  in young adulthood, 99–100
False pride, 69
Falstaff (Verdi), 139

Fame and regret, 161–177
  athletics and, 167–168
  Bacall, Lauren, 172
  Beauvoir, Simone de, 175
  Burnett, Carol, 170–171
  Capote, Truman, 164
  Clift, Montgomery, 162, 163
  Coward, Noel, 174–175
  Cuomo, Mario, 162–163
  Douglas, Kirk, 172
  Dutton, Charles, 176–177
  Fitzgerald, F. Scott, 98–99, 164–166
  Fitzgerald, Zelda, 164, 165, 166
  Fourcade, Marie-Madeleine, 171–172
  Frost, Robert, 173
  Gardner, Ava, 168–169
  Garland, Judy, 161
  Goodson, Mark, 172–173
  Hemingway, Ernest, 172
  "imposter phenomenon," 166–167
  Lancaster, Burt, 170
  Loren, Sophia, 169–170
  Milken, Michael, 163–164
  Miller, Arthur, 173
  O'Brien, Edna, 173–174
  Sheehan, Neil, 174
  Thomas, Dylan, 166
  Williams, Tennessee, 175, 177
Fan's Notes, A (Exley), 13
Fear
  of being laughed at/appearing foolish, 79–80
  of change, 124
  connected to risk-taking in children, 77
  dealing with in children, 78–79
Feminine mystique, 71
Festinger, Leon, 70
Fitzgerald, F. Scott, 98–99, 164–166
Fitzgerald, Zelda, 164, 165, 166
Forgiveness, 129, 146, 151
Fourcade, Marie-Madeleine, 171–172

Franck, Frederick, 140
Freud, Sigmund, 44, 136
Friedan, Betty, 71
Friendship
  men and, 93
  old age and, 158
  value of, 80–81
Fromm, Erich, 48, 49, 55
Frost, Robert, 125, 173

G
Gandhi, Mohandas, 135
Garden of Eden, The (Hemingway), 97
Gardner, Ava, 168–169
Garland, Judy, 161
Gasset, José Ortega y, 193
Generativity, 135–136, 150, 181
Gide, André, 9
Gilligan, Carol, 93
Glass Menagerie, The (Williams), 95
Goodson, Mark, 172–173
Goodwin, Gail, 139
Gould, Roger, 107, 119, 122, 130, 133
Grandparents, 149–151
Greene, Graham, 175–176
Guilt, 8, 38, 142, 184
  cases of, 38–39, 182–184
  reparation and, 38, 39
  See also Altruism; Self-blame.

H
Hamilton, Juan, 156
Harris, Sidney J., 76–77
Hellman, Lillian, 165
Hemingway, Ernest, 97, 172
Henri, Robert, 106, 124
Henry, Jules, 80
Herman, Judith, 61
Heroic impulse, 48
Hero's journey, 48
Herzog (Bellow), 143
Hobbes, Thomas, 77
Holidays and regret, 198–199

Holocaust, 58
Homosexuality, 131–132
Horney, Karen, 10, 33, 34, 69
Hughes, Howard, 168, 172
Humor, 186–189
Hypersensitivity to criticism, 35

I
Idealization
  lost opportunities, 55–56
  love, 118–119
  lovers, 53–55
  self, 34, 69, 189
Illusions
  adolescent, of limitless potential, 102
  autonomy and independence, 13–16
  "de-illusionment," 133
  having no choice, 43, 85
  idealized lost opportunities, 55–56
  idealized love, 53–55, 118–119
  perfect self, 34, 69, 189
  "shoulds," 33
  total freedom, 18
  unrestricted choices, 12–13, 19–20
"Imposter phenomenon," 166–167
Incest victims and repression, 61
Inferno, The (Dante), 125
Instant gratification, 18–19, 179
Intellectualization, 64–66
  case of husband with wife's affair, 65–66

J
James, Henry, 156–157
James, William, 53
Janis, Irving, 112
Jersild, Arthur, 79
Johnson, Samuel, 18

K
Kafka, Franz, 201
Karp, David, 122, 137

Kazan, Elia, 173
Kelley, Kitty, 168
Kinnell, Galway, 118
Kivnick, Janet, 149–150
Kundera, Milan, 113

L
Laing, R. D., 38
Lancaster, Burt, 170
Late adulthood. See Old age.
Lehman, Harvey, 140
Levinson, Daniel, 101, 112, 133
Life assessment/life review, 142–146
  Atwater, Lee, 144–145
  Herzog, 143
  McNamara, Robert, 143–144, 145
  Williams, Tennessee, 175, 177
  See also Self-empowerment worksheet; Self-inventory.
Life magazine, 144
London, Jack, 141
Loren, Sophia, 169–170
Love
  idealized, 53–55, 118–119
  loss of, 15–16, 44–45, 55, 182, 192–193
  middle age and, 117–119
  risk-taking in, 50–51
  sexual expression in old age, 156–158
  unrealistic claims and, 70
"Lovesong of J. Alfred Prufrock, The" (Eliot), 115, 123
Lowenstein, Sophie Freud, 136
Luce, Clare Booth, 46, 52
Luce, Henry, 46

M
Mann, Martin, 112
Marriage
  caretaker instead of partner, 107
  case of dependent wife, 128

case of doctor who married "disguised parent," 107–108
case of intellectualization of husband with wife's affair, 65–66
case of rationalization of dependent wife, 66–67
case of vasectomy and regret, 113–114
case of wife's choice between husband and lover, 181–182
choice made on personal values and, 47
"disguised parent," 107
early and regret, 29–30, 107–108
lack of risk and, 48
O'Brien, Edna and end of her, 173–174
O'Keeffe, Georgia and Alfred Stieglitz, 36–37
unmarried state and regret, 109
woman's career at midlife and, 137
wrong choice of mate and regret, 31–32
Marvell, Andrew, 120
Maslow, Abraham, 53
Maturity, definition, 76–77
May, Rollo, 64
McCarthyism, regret and participants in, 172–173
McElwaine, Robert, 163
McNamara, Robert, 143–144, 145
Men
  altruism in, 181
  middle life and generativity, 136
  regrets related to traditionally "male" characteristics, 93
Merton, Andrew, 86–87
Michelangelo, 139
Middle age
  aging parents and, 135
  assertiveness, new, in, 124–125, 127, 136
  career change in, 122, 124

cases of regret in, 118–119, 121–125
change in, 120, 125, 132
Dante on, 125
"de-illusionment," 133
Eliot, T. S., on, 123
Frost, Robert, on, 125
generativity in, 135–136
goals, clarification of, 120, 130
intellectual and spiritual life in, 129
love, new in, 119
love, past memories of, 117–119
Lowenstein, Sophie Freud, in, 136
mortality, recognition of, 130
parental self-blame in, 133–135
past, confronting our, 120
reassessment in, 117, 119, 125–126
regret about education and careers in, 120–125
truth, realization of, 119–120
youth, loss of, 129–130
Milken, Michael, 163–164
Miller, Alice, 86
Miller, Arthur, 173
Miller, Jean Baker, 93, 180–181
Moustakis, Clark, 78

N
Neugarten, Bernice, 125–126, 127, 129
New York Times, The, 86, 170
  Goodson article, 172–173
  Quindlen column, 145
  survey of young adults, 100
Nietzsche, Friedrich, 162, 187
Nozick, Robert, 109–110
Nussbaum, Martha, 36

O
O'Brien, Edna, 173–174
Obsessive state of regret, 31, 54, 68, 193
  See also Thought stopping.
O'Keeffe, Georgia, 36–37, 104–105, 156

Old age
  beyond regret, moving, 141–142, 145–146, 158
  cases of closure on regret, 152–154
  case of parent and grown child, 148–149
  case of wife's regret in, 147–148
  choice and control, 155
  creativity, resurgence of, 139–140
  forgiveness of self, 151
  Franck, Frederick and, 140
  generativity in, 150
  grandparenthood, 149–151
  happiness in, 146
  health and contentment in, 151–152
  James, Henry and, 156–157
  life assessment/life review, 142–146
  mortality, facing, 140–141
  new interests in, 152, 155–156
  O'Keeffe, Georgia and, 156
  parenting and grown children, 148–149
  pleasure while young and, 146–148
  potential for despair, 142
  quest for personal understanding in, 140
  relationships with friends, 158
  reminiscing in, 145–146
  retirement, 154–155
  sense of spirituality in, 141
  sexual expression in, 156–158
Ozick, Cynthia, 13–14

P
Parade magazine, 169
Parenting
  behavior that causes child pain, 88, 150
  case of aged parent and grown child, 148–149
  case of denial of child's unhappiness, 61–62

  case of daughter separating from mother, 189–190
  case of father with second family, 67
  case of grandparenting, 150–151
  case of parent with handicapped child, 62–64
  cases of self-blame, 134, 173
  children's choices and, 84–87
  children's fear, dealing with, 78
  moral conflicts in choices of, 36
  regret about, in middle age, 133–135
  separation of child from parent, 111–112
  separation of self from child, 86–87
Perfectionism, 19, 33–36, 37, 137
  case of business success and, 34–35
  case of family relationships, 35–36
  definition, 33–34
  humor as defense for, 189
Perkins, Maxwell, 165
Psychotherapy
  case of broken romance and, 192
  case of parent with handicapped child, 62–64
  case of rationalization of dependent wife, 66–67
  case of self-blame and, 26–28
  dreams as therapeutic tool, 62
  regret not identified by clinicians, 31
  task of letting go in, 26–28
  when needed, 200

Q
Quindlen, Anna, 145

R
Rationalization, 66–67
  case of dependent wife, 66–67

case of father with second family, 67

Reality
confronting, 58
unrealistic claims and, 70
See also Defenses, psychological.

Reframing, 192–193

Regret
accepting pain of, 128
anticipatory, 112–115, 189–191
assertiveness and, 43–44
Atwater, Lee, 144–145
behaviors contributing to regret, 199–200
beyond regret, moving, 141–142, 145–146, 158, 177
birthdays/holidays and, 198–199
blindness, willful and, 31–32
cases of, cited, 11–12, 15–16, 18–19, 20, 23–30, 31–32, 34–36, 38–39, 41–43, 44–45, 48–49, 54–56, 95–97, 98, 99–100, 103–104, 105–106, 107–108, 109, 111–112, 113–114, 118–119, 121–125, 126–127, 128, 131–133, 134, 136, 147–148, 150–151, 152–154, 181–183, 187–188, 192–193, 194–197
in childhood, 75–94
Chinese character for, 22
Chinese phrase and, 146
choice and, 8, 10, 30, 71–72
closure on regret, 152–154
contemporary culture and, 10–20
continuum of, 9–10, 30–31, 204
coping with, 22, 30, 32, 62, 72, 179–201
defenses, psychological and, 57–72, 191–192
definition, 7–8
denying, 57, 67, 71, 128
as distinct emotion, 8, 203
fame and, 161–177

guidelines for professional help, 200
James, Henry, and, 156
Luce, Clare Booth and, 46, 52
McNamara, Robert and, 143–144, 145
middle age and, 117–137
obsessive state of, 31, 54, 68, 193
O'Keeffe, Georgia and, 36–37
old age and, 139–158
as positive force, 9, 26, 36, 44, 53, 56, 84, 100, 112–115, 120, 124
self-empowerment worksheet, 205–207
self-image and, 90–91
self-inventory, 3–5, 203–205
success, too early and, 97–100, 163–167
unlived life, 46, 94
unyielding, 68–69
women and, 71, 102–103
writing as therapy and, 175–176
in young adulthood, 95–115
See also Coping with regret; Risk; Self-blame.

Relationships
autonomy and independence in, 13–16
case of broken romance, 192–193
case of brother/sister estrangement, 194–195
case of career over relationship, 95–97
case of delayed divorce, 126–127
case of denial and parent-child estrangement, 59–61
case of humor after rejection, 187–188
case of older parent and grown child, 148, 149
case of perfectionism in family relationships, 35–36

Relationships (*cont.*)
case of relationship before woman's career, 103–104
case of sibling leaving, 182–184
case of widow's regrets, 147–148
Erikson, Erik, on maintaining identity in relationships, 108–109 109
fear of rejection and, 80–81
female self-effacement in, 93–94, 103
idealized lost love, 118–119
idealized lover and failure of, 54–55
intellectualization and, 65–66
old age and, 158
rationalization and, 66–67
regret and clarification of needs, 36
regret and lack of pursuing, 44–45
regrets and wasted, 147–148
Smiley, Jane and, 45
unrealistic claims and, 70
Remorse, 8, 142
Milken, Michael, 163–164
Reparation, 38, 39
Repression, 61–62
incest victims and, 61
Retirement, 154–155, 167–168
Riche, Martha Farnsworth, 100–101
Risk
case of failed attempt and growth, 50–51
case of lack of risk-taking, 48–49
case of living in the moment, 195–197
case of successful risk and growth, 51–52
in childhood, 77–81
dissatisfaction in life and lack of, 48, 172–173
famous people and taking, 162, 170–172
hero's journey and, 48

knowing personal values and, 47
living in the present and, 197
in middle age, 123
"Road Not Taken, The" (Frost), 125
Road not taken, 9, 41
adolescence and, 82
artists and, 106–107
Beauvoir, Simone de, 175
case of giving child up for adoption, 41–43
case of opera career unpursued, 105–106
childhood regret and, 82–87
education and, 45–46, 83–85, 120–125
Frost, Robert, 123
love and, 44–45, 118–119
Luce, Clare Booth and, 46, 52
suffering from, 45
unlived life, 46
Roberts, Michael, 75
Roosevelt, Eleanor, 180
Rosa (Ozick), 13–14
Rossi, Alice, 119
Rubin, Theodore Isaac, 135, 158, 194

S
Sarton, May, 56
Schulberg, Budd, 165
Schweitzer, Albert, 180
Seize the moment, 195–197
Self
accepting responsibility and finding of, 56, 69
adult identity, creating, 101, 115, 167
Baldwin quote on, 41
choices made before discovering, 108
definition, 34
discovering real, 37
Erikson, Erik, on maintaining

identity in relationships, 108–109
"falling apart," 108
Fromm, Erich, on, 55
vs. idealized image, 34, 69, 189
Maslow, Abraham, on inner nature, 53
Self-blame, 21–32
action taken/not taken and, 29–31, 46, 179
bitterness and, 23–26
cases/examples of, 23–29, 54–56, 85, 111, 192–193, 197–198
confronting, 53
death of loved one and, 26–28
forgiveness of self, 39
inappropriate, 22–23, 28–29, 100
language of, 44
mediation, in middle age, 125
parental, 133–135
soothing, 181, 197
Self-compassion, 32–39, 44, 46, 64, 135, 142, 152, 181, 191, 192
Self-deception. See Defenses, psychological.
Self-empowerment worksheet, 205–207
Self-esteem, 8
in children, 80
infidelity in marriage and, 126
looks and, 168
success and, 44, 162, 167, 168
Self-image, and regret in children, 90–91
Self-inventory, 3–5
scoring, 204
Self-pity, 8, 22, 124, 155
Selye, Hans, 53
Seneca, 161
Shakespeare, William, x
Shames, Lawrence, 166–167
Shaw, George Bernard, 98
Shaw, Irwin, 167
Sheehan, Neil, 174

Sinatra, Frank, 168
Smiley, Jane, 45
Solitude, 81
Einstein, Alfred, and, 81
Sorrow, 8, 10
Southern Family, A (Goodwin), 139
Stafford, William, 7
Stegner, Wallace, 155
Stieglitz, Alfred, 36–37
Storr, Anthony, 81, 140
"Story of Our Lives, The" (Strand), 117
Strand, Mark, 117
Strauss, Richard, 139
Stress
altruism and dealing with, 180
cognitive dissonance and, 70–71
effective defenses and, 180, 191–192
eustress, 53
person as source of, 62
positive, 53
of regret, 58
Success
career and, 122
early and regret, 97–100, 163–167
Fitzgerald, F. Scott, and, 98–99, 164–166
as kind of death, 177
and regret, 13, 44, 161–177
in young adulthood, 97–100
See also Fame and regret.
Sudden, Robert, 8
Suppression, 184–186
Surrender the need to be right, 194–195
Szasz, Thomas, 85–86

T
Talmud, 181
Teaching, dissatisfaction in career, 122–125

Tender Is the Night (Fitzgerald), 164–165

Tennyson, Alfred Lord, 179

Therapy, professional, when needed, 200

See also Psychotherapy.

Thomas, Dylan, 166

Thought stopping, 193–194

Tillich, Paul, 158

Time magazine, 46

McNamara interview, 143–144

report on young adult choices, 101

survey of young adults, 100

"To His Coy Mistress" (Marvell), 120

"Turning against oneself" (Freud), 44

Turning against the self, 62–64

case of parent with handicapped child, 62–64

"Tyranny of the Shoulds" (Horney), 33, 35

U

University of Arizona, study on priorities and regrets, 45

University of California, study of self-image, 91

Unyielding regret, 68–69

case of unmarried daughter, 68

Updike, John, 90

V

Vaillant, George, 185

Values

case/personal example of choice made on, 47

cognitive dissonance and, 70–71

contemporary, 11–13, 15, 16, 18, 53, 97–100, 109, 129–130

evolving childhood, 77, 80–81, 88

friendship and, 80–81

marriage, modern and, 108

personal system of, 20, 46, 47, 94, 106, 130

risk and, 47–49

self and, 34

value judgments by children, 87–88

Vasectomy, and regret, 113–114

Verdi, Giuseppe, 139

W

Walpole, Horace, 156

Waves, The (Woolf), 119

Wechsler, Rabbi Harlan, 134

Wharton, Edith, 71

"When We Two Parted" (Byron), 118

Williams, Tennessee, 95, 175, 177

Wolfe, Thomas, 62

Women

aging and, 168–170

altruism/devaluation of altruism, 180–181

career success and marriage, 173–174

childlessness, regret and, 95–97, 126

conditioned dependency in, 127–128

female self-effacement and regret, 93–94

generativity in, 181

midlife and assertivensss, 136–137

passive-aggressive behavior in, 94

regret and feminine mystique, 71

sexual desire and aging, 157–158

survey of young adult, 102

young adult, gender-influenced choices of, 102–103

Woolf, Virginia, 21, 119

Y

Yeats, William Butler, 39

Young adulthood

adult consciousness in, 112

biological state of, 97
choices in, 96–97, 101–102, 105
demographic study of choices by, 100–101
early choices now regretted, 107–109
effective decision-making guidelines, 112–115
failure in, 101
Fitzgerald, F. Scott in, 98–99
maintaining identity in relationships, 108–109
O'Keeffe, Georgia in, 104–105
regret, cases of in, 95–97, 98–100, 103–104, 105–106, 107–109

report on choices of, 101
separation from parents and, 111–112
success, early in, 97–100, 163–167
survey of, 100
transition from adolescence to adulthood, time needed, 101
women in, 102–103
Youth
  beauty and, 168–169
  definition by Chesterton, 137
  regret and loss of, 129–130

Z
Zoom lens ability, 109–110